CONFESSIONS
OF A HEADMASTER

CONFESSIONS
OF A HEADMASTER

❧

Paul F. Cummins

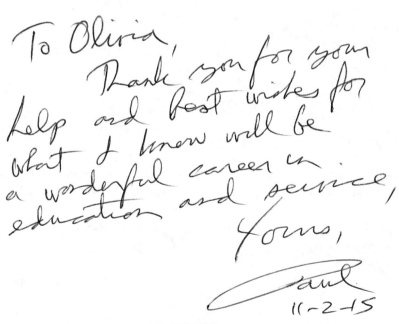

To Olivia,
Thank you for your
help and best wishes for
what I know will be
a wonderful career in
education and service,
Yours,
Paul
11-2-15

XENO

Book design and layout by Selena Trager
Photographs by Shelby Duncan, and from the private collection of Paul and Mary Ann Cummins

Library of Congress Cataloging-in-Publication Data
Cummins, Paul F., 1937–
  Confessions of a headmaster / Paul F. Cummins.—First edition.
    pages cm
  Includes bibliographical references.
  ISBN 978-1-939096-40-1 (pbk. : alk. paper)
  1. Cummins, Paul F., 1937–
  2. Educators—United States—Biography.
  3. School principals—United States—Biography.
  4. Education—United States—Anecdotes. I. Title.
  LA2317.C87A3 2015
  371.20092—dc23
  [B]
                    2015023373

The National Endowment for the Arts, the Los Angeles County Arts Commission, the Los Angeles Department of Cultural Affairs, the Dwight Stuart Youth Fund, the Pasadena Arts & Culture Commission and the City of Pasadena Cultural Affairs Division, Sony Pictures Entertainment, and the Ahmanson Foundation partially support Red Hen Press.

First Edition
XENO Books is an imprint of Red Hen Press, Pasadena, CA
www.redhen.org/xeno

ACKNOWLEDGMENTS

The decision to write an autobiography originated with a desire to pass on to my children a more comprehensive story than my father left behind. I was encouraged in this effort by my daughters, Liesl, Julie, Anna, and Emily, and, of course, my wife, Mary Ann. Their contributions to my life and this book pervade the spirit of its contents.

My former assistant, Jackie Stehr, endured draft after draft (as well as daft after daft) and made many, many helpful suggestions and corrections.

Nancy Bryan read an early draft and applied her sharp and wise rake to weed out unnecessary, redundant, and excessive stories and feelings. She rescued me from sailing into troubled waters.

Several other friends read the entire manuscript—in particular, Vicky Schorr, Kelly Kagan Law, and Carla Malden, and each gave honest, generous, and invaluable suggestions. Also, David Rose of Red Hen Press provided a meticulous and helpful editing job, as did my daughter, Anna.

Two friends gave me the extraordinary gift of a line-by-line stylistic editing and chapter-by-chapter commentary on the content and structure of the book. To Leslie Gilbert Lurie and Kristin Herbert I offer a hug and a heartfelt thank you.

DEDICATION

In a sense, I would like to dedicate this book to everyone mentioned within, for each is an integral strand in the fabric of my life.

Specifically, I want to honor the other seven founding board members of Crossroads School: Rhoda Makoff, Ed Kaufman, Ken Ruby, and—in memoriam—Mel Edelstein, Linda Elstad, Gerry Sherman, and Peter Swerling. In reality, the late Irene Jerison was also part of this group. Together we created a school of which we can all be proud.

Frank Grisanti (now deceased) was a surrogate father, mentor, and superb board chair at the beginning of my days at St. Augustine's. As Crossroads evolved, four other board chairs were both mentors and dear friends: Chuck Boxenbaum, Shirley Garber, Lucy Ann Geiselman, and Nat Trives. My debt to each is enormous.

I would be remiss not to mention a few other individuals, even though doing so always runs the risk of omitting other major players in one's life. Nevertheless, Herb Alpert, Jack Zimmerman, Warren Spaeth, John Carswell, Nat Reynolds, Peter Levitt, Elizabeth Keyser, Herbert Zipper (in memoriam), Michele Hickey (in memoriam), and Kelly Kagan Law have been irreplaceable friends.

Family is at the center of each of our lives, and I feel blessed to have had the two loving parents that fortune bequeathed to me. My late sister, Mimi, her husband, Ken, and his new wife, Ann, and their extended family belong in this pantheon. Finally, Liesl; Julie and Paul, Conner and Jake; Anna, Marcus and Avani; Emily, Adam, Della, and Dax; and, of course, my muse and my mate, Mary Ann, complete this circle of love.

How small a part of time they share
that are so wondrous sweet and fair.

—Edmund Waller

CONTENTS

The Road to Becoming a Headmaster 1937–1970

**New Roads and New Visions
1990 Onward**

EPILOGUE

A PERSONAL, BRIEF, IDIOSYNCRATIC, AND
LIFE-CHANGING BIBLIOGRAPHY

INTRODUCTION

I HAD NEVER HEARD OF Paul Cummins when I filled out an application for my son to join the kindergarten class at Crossroads, the first school he co-founded, which went on to become a nationally respected and beloved institution. Not that he and it weren't already famous at the time I turned in the forms; our son was one of hundreds in the applicant pool. I didn't know that, because I was a blithe parent, intent on tunneling deeper into my own field (literary fiction) and feared that reading books about parenting or education would mom-ify me and somehow exempt me from the running to make something beautiful.

We didn't expect to send our son to Crossroads, anyway. Experience in three pre-schools, two on this coast, one in the east, had convinced us that our child thrived in structure. I was a mother most content when my child was strapped into a stroller. I liked the aesthetic of children perched on wooden desks in rows, wearing white collared uniform shirts. I saw nothing wrong with memorization, especially of Shakespeare, Milton, and Chaucer.

Nonetheless, despite our reservations, our son did end up a member of the Crossroads kindergarten class for the simple reason that we were rejected by every other Los Angeles private school. Our precociously verbal son used his acumen to say "I don't want to go to your damn school," to a former nun who'd made the emphatic point during orientation that the one thing she would not tolerate was bad language.

Crossroads, we were told, did not believe in interviewing five-year-olds. This turned out to be a very good thing for us. Once I knew the school culture, I guessed that Crossroads didn't believe in the nice language/bad language dichotomy either.

But even so, we did not start our family's Crossroads journey as converts. In the twelve (should we just say years because I think actually it would be thirteen or more—our daughter is still at xrds!) years that followed, we were convinced that education could be both rigorous and joyful.

Except for the absence of uniforms and desks in rows, Crossroads turned out to be everything I'd hoped for and hadn't expected: an academically ambitious hub that thrived on intellectual discussion rather than rote learning. Poetry was read, written and yes, even memorized and recited aloud. Most importantly, an ever-present undercurrent seemed to teach morality every day, in the course of play and work. That awareness made an active pulse. *You can't say you can't play* was an enforced rule.

Confessions of a Headmaster, by Paul Cummins, the legendary educator who brought his first school (eventually named Crossroads) from the brink of closing down in bankruptcy to national prominence, is the chronicle of a group endeavor. Cummins recruited teachers with a passion for the subjects they taught, and the school they created together treated the arts, athletics, community service, human development, and environmental studies as subjects every bit as "solid" as the so-called core curriculum. This is also the story of a man who brought the romance and joy back into teaching at a time when education was (and remains) a field of constant national controversy, and our most popular books have titles with militarist references, such as *The Teacher Wars*.

Crossroads is still housed in a group of industrial buildings clustered around an alley, which has, as one supporter fondly said, "all the ambience of a tire factory," proving that the essence of education does not depend upon any particular acreage of manicured athletic fields or brick and ivy buildings.

The school's success may have something to do with Crossroads's budgetary commitment, from the very beginning, to allocate at least ten percent for financial aid and with a principal who knew every single pupil's name. It certainly had something to do with the fact that Paul Cummins was the only Los Angeles educator to immediately accept and welcome the Glaser kids, who had been infected during the early years of the AIDS epidemic by their mother, who herself had been infected during a blood transfusion.

During the Cummins years, a weekly assembly began—with candles and music—and children of all ages speaking. By the time of fifth- and sixth-grade graduations, teachers discovered the children were no longer nervous speaking in front of audiences. Crossroads sponsored faculty versus student water-balloon fights, the ritual dunking of the headmaster in a rented vat of water, and Jell-O wrestling.

Goofiness was not only allowed but encouraged. Annual pajama days and bring-your-dog days became long-standing traditions. Fun and joy were valued, not feared.

In his *Confessions*, Cummins talks frankly about difficult things: he defines the "F word" as "fundraising" and once turned down half a million dollars from a family whose only stipulation was that he slip in two of their children. The school was full, period.

He tells a story about meeting a potential donor, hoping to bring her to tears with his philosophy of education. Instead, she told him that what really sold her were his shabby clothes. "She thought that any head of school with so little concern for his appearance must be a good educator."

The part of the book I cherish most is Paul's personal history, what you might call *The Portrait of an Educator as a Young Man.*

Paul comes from a street in Brentwood where some of Crossroads's wealthiest families still live, in a house on an acre and a half, graced with orange trees and roses. (The house sold for $5,800,000 in 2012, one instance of the kind of frank detail Paul reveals in these pages—in the service of emphasizing the role privilege plays in the kind of education available to America's children, he uses his own example.) Several Mexican workers cared for the grounds, as well as a Japanese gardener, and the family was served by an African-American woman whom the Cummins parents referred to as their "colored maid."

His childhood was a kind of idyll: he fed squirrels at the kitchen window and made balsa wood Flying Tiger airplanes. He went to a public California junior high that employed four PE teachers and full-time specialists in music, art, the-ater, wood shop, electrical shop, drafting, and crafts. Today, in our nation's public schools, virtually none of these specialties are represented. Paul took his leather football to bed with him every night, and his sister shrieked when Frank Sinatra came on the radio.

His parents were secretly relieved when FDR died. His father drove a gold Ca-dillac El Dorado, his mother a white Cadillac Coupe de Ville, and Paul asked them to drop him off two blocks away from school. He'd befriended some Latino kids and didn't want his wealth to be apparent.

He attended Crossroads's rival private high school, not incidentally called Har-vard (now Harvard Westlake), where he and his peers drank beer and only beer at parties, drove around Los Angeles after midnight, made out during drive-in movies watching Doris Day, Jimmy Stewart, and June Allyson, and graduated virgins.

"I didn't read. I think I read two novels in all my high school years, and I gener-ally relied on Classic Comics when writing book reports on Dickens or Heming-way. I was interested in sports and girls—in that order."

Yet despite all that, in 1955, Cummins drove his own Chevy Bel Air from Brentwood to Palo Alto, to attend Stanford. His dad had told him "It's great preparation for business."

He'd intended to play football, but after a shoulder injury early in the season, he realized he was not good enough to play at the collegiate level. It was then that his real education began.

"Here I was, culturally semi-illiterate, possessing an average intellect, studying at Stanford University. I was there only because I was white, from the lower echelons of the upper class, and had come from a private school with a father who could pull strings and pay full tuition."

But if entitlement got him in, Cummins did not take to college in the manner of a spoiled son. He fell under the spell of a professor named Otis Pease and took every class of his that was offered. He wrote down the names of all the books Pease recommended and spent his whole allowance on them, books he has even now on his shelves. He talks about opening Arthur S. Link's *American Epoch* from time to time, not just for information but as "a sort of pilgrimage to an important shrine." The shrine commemorates the dawning of his intellectual identity. Richard Hofstadter became a hero to the young history major.

"My heroes were no longer just Joe DiMaggio," he writes. "I sympathize with parents who fear that education will cause their children to reject parental values. All I can say to them is 'Yes, I understand; it has been known to happen' (and I silently add, 'to me')."

In a letter to his father from Stanford, Cummins wrote:

> . . . the thought of building a school someday myself is with me every day. I constantly dream of building and leading a school where students are encouraged and helped to: seek the meaning of life, read and discuss the world's great literature and music, to speak a foreign language and not just memorize vocabulary words which will be forgotten in a few years' time, to have a knowledge of current events, . . . and so on into the night.

Most people, after creating a thriving community would stay on as headmaster for their working lives. But Paul Cummins decided to leave others to run his magical (and by then prestigious) school, in order to commit his time and energy to the shakier prospect of educating our most needy students.

A question nagged him perpetually: "If government doesn't look out for the poor and disenfranchised, who will?" He writes that he's repeatedly asked this question of his students, colleagues, and acquaintances for the past fifty-one years and has yet to receive a satisfactory answer.

While still at Crossroads, he went out to visit local public schools and was shocked by what he found, even in the relatively wealthy sections of Los Angeles.

"I found schools with virtually no PE teachers, no arts teachers, no reading or math specialists, no librarians, and no counselors.

In one particular school, the third-grade teacher had begun a school year in September with thirty students, and by March she had thirty different students: a 100 percent turnover! 'My God,' I said to the principal, 'how can you teach under such conditions?'

'You tell me,' she responded."

Paul's response was to launch PS Arts, a program to bring working artists into the public schools in 1993, and to found the New Visions Foundation in 1994 (renamed in 2014 as the Coalition for Engaged Education), which founded New Roads School, an independent school that dedicates forty percent of its tuition revenue to need-based financial aid and cultivates a diversity that goes way beyond race, as well as Camino Nuevo Charter Academy in 2000, New Village Charter School (the only single-sex charter granted by LAUSD, a high school for pregnant and parenting young women), and an educational program at Camp Gonzales, in 2001, whose alumni—formerly incarcerated young men—continue to achieve unprecedented success. He co-created a program to connect foster youth with quality educational opportunities and stay with them, offering various kinds of support through college, until they have achieved positive, self-sustaining lives. The Coalition's latest endeavors focus on the underserved children and youth in Lennox, California, an unincorporated area near LAX.

With his outrage at our society's divisions of "expensive children and "cheap children," he writes that "retirement is simply out of the question."

Thank goodness for us. The Talmud says that thirty-six righteous people save the world.

Paul Cummins is endlessly self-deprecating and modest in these pages, not in any smarmy fake way, but out of a kind and democratic vision. He tells us that his IQ was most likely average, that in college he was a B student and it took him longer to learn than many of his quick classmates at Stanford. Looking at Crossroads, he ruminates: "To this day, I wonder how I could have been responsible for creating such an environment. I am a rather private, quiet, book-loving person. Perhaps this atmosphere just 'happened,' and I was a fortunate bystander."

In the end, after such a successful career, after changing the lives of so many students, Cummins describes a moment when, teaching at his old high school, he was looking around the basement files for a student record and found his own SAT scores.

"When I discovered the scores, I was a teacher, a holder of several degrees, twenty-five years old, and feeling fairly self-confident in my chosen field. I was utterly shocked! The scores were amazingly low. I stared at them in disbelief, because now I was a college counselor, and I knew what they meant. Those numbers hit me between the eyes. I was depressed for weeks. Was I really that stupid? How could I be teaching when all my students were more intelligent than I?

"Today, with my SAT scores, I would never have gone to Stanford."

Paul Cummins is a revolutionary—not only declaring that wealthy and poor students should be granted the riches of intellectual civilization—he insists on a democratization of learning itself. The pleasures of our artistic and intellectual legacy should not only be given to the wealthy, nor should they be bequeathed only to our A students, our high scorers, our geniuses.

These gifts are part of our intellectual commons—and well deserved by every single child.

—Mona Simpson

"The time has come," the walrus said, "to talk of many things . . ."

—Lewis Carroll

The Creation of Crossroads
1970 Onward

"The world's
a dream." Basho said,
"not because that dream's
a falsehood, but because it's
truer than it seems."

—Richard Wilbur

PROLOGUE:

A New Beginning

The woods are lovely, dark and deep,
But I have promises to keep,
And miles to go before I sleep,
And miles to go before I sleep.

—Robert Frost,
"Stopping by Woods on a Snowy Evening"

MY THIRTY-TWO YEARS AT CROSSROADS School were coming to an end. This spring evening of 2002 at the Miramar Hotel in Santa Monica was to be the farewell celebration. Mary Ann and I picked up my ninety-two-year-old mother at her senior home nearby and drove to the hotel along the Palisades bluff overlooking the Pacific Ocean as the sun, almost on cue, was setting.

I had been the lead founder of Crossroads, its headmaster for twenty-two years. I had stayed on an additional ten years as president, focusing on outreach programs. But thirty-two years seemed enough, and I felt it was time to move on to new ventures. At first my family tried to talk me out of it—none of them could envision the school without me. For my daughters, Anna and Emily, Crossroads had been the hub of much of their life's wheel with me as a daily presence at the school. Mary Ann, who planned to stay at the school indefinitely, could not imagine my not being there.

The farewell celebration was upon us, and as we drove up to the hotel, I found my stomach in knots and my eyes already beginning to sting.

The forty-third president of the United States also came to speak—well, actually it was Harry Shearer doing a hilarious impersonation in which he pledged, along with his Catholic brethren, "to leave no child's behind" (which engendered an audible groan of laughter) and that as "The Educationist President" he would serve education "all over the world—and elsewhere."

Poignant moments came when two alums took the stage. First was Danielle de Niese, an international opera star who offered a rendition of a favorite song of mine, "Time After Time." The second was Ahrin Mishan. Ahrin was a former sort of "Westside orphan" who came to Crossroads in the seventh grade and lived with our family for several years. Because Ahrin stayed away from home as much as he did, he had few places and spaces of his own. He was always a guest in someone else's home.

As he recalled it, one day I brought him into the living room where I had emptied out a long shelf in our floor-to-ceiling bookcase and said to him, "Ahrin, this is for your books for as long as we live here." To him it was an unforgettable moment and, of course, a reminder of what gives a sense of meaning to life.

When one era in your life ends, inevitably you reflect on how it began. For me the Crossroads era and my foray into progressive education began in late May of 1970 when I was asked to apply for the headmaster position at St. Augustine's by-the-Sea Episcopal School. I even remember one of my first visits to the school.

CHAPTER 1

The New Headmaster at St. Augustine's by-the-Sea

An autobiography is the story of how a man thinks he lived.

—Henny Youngman

I WAS THE VISITING DIGNITARY, the prospective headmaster (now head of school) being ushered from classroom to classroom. As I entered the third-grade classroom, the teacher, a pale replica of someone Ed Wood might have cast as Bela Lugosi's wife, motioned with her two hands as if scooping up sand, and the children—arranged in five neat rows of five each—rose in unison. One more scoop, and they said, in that sing-songy, sassy way children have when adults order them to do something, "Good morning, Dr. Cummins!" The teacher frowned—one student had lagged behind by a millisecond. She scooped again, and again they chirped, this time with perfect precision, "Good morning, Dr. Cummins!" I cringed.

This was the school in microcosm: children were being trained to be miniature adults in a rather sterile and joyless process. I hadn't set foot in an elementary school since the day I graduated from sixth grade in June 1949. Yet here I was, in

1

May of 1970, at thirty-two years old, about to become headmaster of this school, St. Augustine's by-the-Sea Episcopal School located in Santa Monica.

I knew almost nothing about elementary education. I hadn't expected to get the job offer; after all, I didn't even have an elementary school credential, and, furthermore, I was too liberal for this place. What I didn't know was that the Board of Directors was desperate: it was May, and the school needed a headmaster immediately. If members of the board had visited me in my then-current job as assistant head of the progressive Oakwood School in North Hollywood, I would never have been considered for the position. They would have seen a tableau out of the 1960s: long-haired kids playing guitars on the lawn, singing Bob Dylan songs, dressed in the sloppy uniform of the times: tie-dyed T-shirts, faded Levi's with holes in the knees, and such. However, the selection committee never came to see me in my habitat, nor did they explore my politics, but they were impressed by my USC PhD as well as my Stanford BA and Harvard MAT, and they liked that I had once been a sort-of Episcopalian.

Nat Reynolds, my close friend, former colleague, and a St. Augustine's trustee, had convinced the decision-makers that I was the right choice. After my initial tour of the school, I called him to ask why the children were required to walk from class to class in columns of two with their hands clasped behind their backs. For a moment he was silent—I suspected this was news to him. He quick-wittedly retorted, "Well, I suppose it cuts down on masturbation."

During this courtship period, I wrote the selection committee a letter outlining ten actions I would take, if hired, to make St. Augustine's a better place. These included:

- adding a rich arts program to the curriculum
- admitting a more diverse student population
- adding electives to the course offerings
- and moving to a more open classroom design, with learning stations and individualized programs of instruction.

I figured that any one of these suggestions would kill my candidacy. But other factors prevailed: primarily, it was late in the spring, and they were near panic, so I was offered the job.

Frank Grisanti, the chairman of the school's Board of Directors and the vestry (the church board) as well, was a powerful man who gradually became my friend. Our politics diverged widely, but we liked each other and he took on a fatherly role, advising and occasionally reprimanding me. He was a Vince Lombardi look-alike as well as act-alike. One sharp look from Frank would shatter glass: you just didn't mess with him. For some reason, he decided to back me, and even when he must have disagreed with my policies, he supported me and quieted his anxious fellow board members. I would never have survived my first two turbulent years as head-master without his full confidence. And even so, it was touch and go!

There was a personal foreground to my unlikely debut at St. Augustine's. Some-time during the fall of 1967, I had been invited to a dinner party where I met a bright, dynamic lady named Rhoda Makoff, who had a PhD in biochemistry and was deeply interested in education. As we began talking, we found ourselves in instant agreement that most public schools were rigid, test-driven, arts-deprived, intellectually thin, and, overall, rather sterile institutions. There was an underly-ing set of assumptions about the purpose of education that pretty much reflected materialistic, conservative, anti-intellectual mainstream "Americanism." Schools, Rhoda and I agreed, need not be this way, but to create such a school would prove, as we later learned, to be an uphill climb. We speculated: wouldn't it be exciting to start a school—maybe even together? It was a conversation probably helped along by a few glasses of wine, but it was a conversation I remembered. Consequently, when I was offered and accepted the job at St. Augustine's, Rhoda was the first per-son I called. I said, "I know you're Jewish, and I know this isn't exactly a new school, but it is an opportunity to create something new. So, how about joining me as my assistant head, teaching some science, and having some fun?" She agreed, and we set about designing a curriculum and hiring faculty.

When I was hired in late May of 1970, Frank had told me to look over my fac-ulty of seventeen (eight full-time and nine part-time) and to determine which ones I wanted to keep. In this school, three were popular and politically "untouchable": kindergarten, first grade, and the Spanish teacher; the other fourteen were up to me. I observed them all, and Rhoda and I decided to fire all fourteen. In retrospect, I probably violated every rule taught in management schools, but I now believe my ignorance was a blessing. Rather than trying to coax, cajole, and change fourteen people, many of whom would probably have been staunchly resistant to my ideas, I made a clean sweep and started the new season with my own team. I made some hiring mistakes and replaced a few of these at the end of the first year, but in rela-tively short order we had assembled a first-rate faculty and an excellent program.

When we began assembling our faculty, I asked Rhoda whether she knew of any music teachers we might interview. Music was an integral part of my life, and I wanted it integrated into our curriculum as well. Rhoda had heard of a terrific piano teacher in the Santa Monica Canyon named Mary Ann Erman, so I called her and told her I was looking for an elementary music teacher. She already had a job teaching something called "Orffschulwerk" in the Bellflower school system, but she invited me over for dinner to introduce me to two other Orff teachers and said I could take my pick. "What is Orff?" I inquired, never even having heard the word before. "Come to dinner and find out," she answered. So I did.

I arrived at 550 E. Rustic Road and was greeted by a startlingly beautiful, curly-haired blonde whose warmth and vitality were palpable. It became clear rather quickly that she knew a great deal about music and cared deeply about education. But first, as I later learned about Mary Ann, first must come dinner, and a gourmet one at that—prepared by Mary Ann, herself.

The dinner was fantastic—as all of Mary Ann's dinners are, I was to learn. After dinner she set up the Orff instruments in the living room and conducted a mock mini-class in Orffschulwerk—a method of teaching music to children. I was so impressed by this introduction to Carl Orff that I became a devotee, and now (more than forty years later) believe it to be the most effective way to teach music to children. Orff, who composed the world-renowned Carmina Burana, traveled the world, studying how music is taught, then designed his own comprehensive method that combined the elements of music (melody, rhythm, harmony) with body movement and language—often nursery rhymes and children's poetry. It is a hands-on, experiential process, and children adore playing the instruments especially designed by Orff (xylophones, hand drums, etc.). While learning the technical skills of reading music and playing various instruments, children are also given the chance to improvise their own melodies and musical ideas and to play in an ensemble. It is a magical, unforgettable experience for them.

After the "class" was over, it was clear to me that Mary Ann was the star of the group, so the next day I called and implored her to take the job. She resisted, but I had two things in my favor: she was a divorced single parent who hated the two-hour round trip to Bellflower each day, and she was dissatisfied with the principal of the local public school her two daughters, Julie and Liesl, would be attending the following year. So I made her an offer she couldn't refuse—free tuition for her two daughters at St. Augustine's. Somewhat reluctantly, she agreed to set up and teach an Orff program. We hired two other music teachers: Mary Ann taught kindergarten and first and second grades; the others taught grades three and four and grades five and six, respectively. They were a wonderful trio and, under Mary Ann's guidance, set up a superb music program. The children were enthralled from day one.

On one occasion, during her first year at the school, I observed Mary Ann teach an Orff class. It was pure magic. The session had everything: a beginning, a middle, and an end; a sequential design with A leading to B leading to C; structure, yet time for improvisation; and clear pedagogical goals that also allowed for the children's creativity. Mostly, I was astounded by her gaiety and passion, her musicality, and her ability to enter a child's world while staying focused on her teaching objectives. I went to my office, called Nat Reynolds, and told him, "I've just witnessed the best teaching I've ever seen, at any grade level, anywhere." I didn't know it at the time, but I was praising the future mother of my two daughters. All that, however, would come later.

I was also fortunate in being hired so late because most of the changes I made took place over the summer when no one was around. By the time parents returned in September, the damage had already been done. That summer of 1970 turned out to be hectic. Besides hiring fourteen new teachers, I set about implementing all the features of my "if-you-hire-me-here's-what-I'll-do" list. I didn't consult any management books or experts; I was full of a youthful drive to act. Prudence would have dictated getting to know the community, gradually gaining community support, and making a few gradual changes the first year. Instead, I made radical changes—almost all of them at once. Surprisingly enough, it worked. The initial storm was furious, but it was over swiftly, and a brand-new school emerged. But, I am getting ahead of my story.

After the faculty was in place, the summer of 1970 presented one big surprise and one major challenge. The surprise was the rector of St. Augustine's. The Reverend S. Hoggard had interviewed me and encouraged me to take the job. He had formerly been an assistant to the radical Bishop James Pike of Grace Cathedral in San Francisco and was himself a progressive thinker in politics, social issues, and theology. Together, he told me, we would do exciting work in transforming the church and school. He was a silver-haired, silver-tongued guy, and I was impressed. I looked forward to our work together. In early July, I went off to Deerfield Academy in Massachusetts to attend a conference-workshop for new heads of schools. When I returned ten days later, Hoggard had resigned. I was stunned. It seemed that there must have been behind-the-scene machinations and problems of which I knew nothing, and though he rescinded his resignation in August and returned to his post, he quit again for good before Christmas. Furthermore, I saw little of him in the fall of 1970.

So I found myself responsible for five chapels a week—at the beginning of every school day. Soon the children were calling me "Father Cummins."

The new enrollment included many Jewish families whom I had reassured that chapel would not be excessively Christian. Hoggard had told me he would help design and carry out humanistic chapel services. Thus, in September, Jewish parents sat on one side of the church vigilantly observing, while the "old guard" Christian parents of the school sat on the other side, closely scrutinizing what went on to be sure that their good old-fashioned religion was not going to be watered down by this "liberal upstart" new headmaster. Needless to say, chapels were a juggling act of poetry readings and various children's activities that were unsatisfactory for many—except the children, who liked the new life they saw being breathed into the school.

The major challenge of that summer was enrollment. When I became headmaster in May, only 100 children were slated to return; a fully enrolled school would be 175. I hired teachers at salaries above the previous year's, raised tuition from $500 to $750 for the year (by the way, in 2014-15, the elementary school tuition is $29,159), and based the budget on a fully enrolled school. I had two months to enroll seventy-five new students or I would crash and burn. The seventy-fifth and final enrollee signed up in late August—Rhoda and I had just barely made it. There were a few unwitting helpers along the way. One was a local public elementary school principal who offended parents right and left with her rigid and high-handed methods, which drove a number of disaffected parents to my office door. Also, a few "old guard" parents who got wind of the changes I was planning began grousing about me publicly, which caused outsiders to think, "If those people think it's so bad, maybe we should look into it."

So September arrived at this "Episcopal school" with a religiously more diverse staff, a student body of 175 with colorful new names and a rainbow of ethnicities, and a new administration. In addition, we presented a child-centered, arts-infused, open-structured curriculum—far from the norm. We set up learning stations in each classroom where groups of two to four students would work, theoretically, according to their own individual skill levels instead of having all twenty-five kids do the same exercise simultaneously. While this is common today, in 1970 it was perceived as radical. At first, it was frenetic. Students who were used to a strict, rigid, and even repressive atmosphere reacted to the new freedoms with exuberance and, at times, wild behavior. Discipline problems surfaced in a school where none had existed before. "See," the naysayers neighed, "this progressive stuff doesn't work." Some of our teachers even came to doubt our new approaches, and some urged returning to the stricter methods of the past.

Rhoda and I held firm. "Give it a chance," we insisted; the students need to be taught how to be self-disciplined. At meeting after meeting with parents, Rhoda and I promoted the notion that creativity, the use of the imagination, and the development of artistic self-expression are as important to children as the Three Rs. Long before Howard Gardner formulated his then seven kinds of intelligence, I was convinced that that the school's curriculum needed to make room for the expression of each child's uniqueness. Some parents were skeptical but receptive;

others were hostile and removed their children from the school. Fortunately, a few were delighted to find a voice reinforcing their own notions that childhood was a precious, unique experience.

The dichotomy in parental attitudes was most striking in the kindergarten. At Frank Grisanti's recommendation—and against my own preference—I retained the "old" kindergarten teacher. She was not only chronologically old but had certainly seen better days as a teacher as well. Nevertheless, because she was strict and insisted on orderly drills, neatness, and politeness, many parents found her entirely satisfactory. Her classroom was tidy and quiet—an adult's vision of what is good for children, except for two crucial ingredients: it lacked imagination and creativity.

It didn't take the new families long to see what I saw. Within two to three weeks, they began coming to see me. "Paul," they would say, "we share your vision for the school, but we can't subject our child to this kindergarten. You've got to do something—soon!" So here I was between the proverbial rock and hard place: thirteen old-guard families "loved" the teacher; twelve new families threatened to leave if I didn't make a change. What to do? I had a stroke of, well, perhaps not genius, but at least radical pragmatism. I invoked the wisdom of Solomon and decided to cut the class in half and create a second kindergarten. I didn't have an extra classroom, so I bought the new teacher, Barbara Sternlight, a big cedar chest in which to store her materials and scheduled her in one corner of the assembly hall. It certainly wasn't ideal, but it salvaged the year and bought me some time. Fortunately, at the end of the year, the "old gal" retired. (As Lefty Gomez once said, "I'd rather be lucky than good.")

In many ways, those days of 1970 seem a lifetime removed from today. Apollo 13 was launched from Cape Kennedy, Salvador Allende was elected president of Chile, the U.S. Army accused soldiers of war crimes at the Vietnamese village of My Lai, and four students were killed at Kent State. But that era's educational issues in America were just like today's. "Back to basics," national standards, cutbacks in funding for the National Endowment for the Arts, and budget cuts for the arts are all new-millennium expressions of the same hostility to the arts and blindness to educational inequities I confronted in the 1970s. Today, as then, politicians, journalists, and citizens-at-large still seem more concerned with test scores than with nurturing the spirits of children.

When I first became headmaster of St. Augustine's, I began a remedial course of instruction in the theory of early education by reading all the new books I could get my hands on: Jonathan Kozol's *Death at an Early Age*; John Holt's *How Children Learn* and *How Children Fail*; Charles E. Silberman's *Crisis in the Classroom*; A.S. Neill's *Summerhill*; George B. Leonard's *Education and Ecstasy*; Herbert Kohl's *36*

Children; Ivan Illich's *Deschooling Society*; Frances G. Wickes's *The Inner World of Childhood*; and Herbert Read's *Education Through Art*. Many of these writers wrote in reaction against the educational conservatism of other writers such as Arthur Bestor, Hyman Rickover, and James D. Koerner. They were a new breed of progressives, and I found myself in instant agreement with what I read. John Holt wrote, "A child is most intelligent when the reality before him arouses in him a high degree of attention, interest, concentration, involvement—in short, when he cares most about what he is doing [and comes] to think and say, 'I see it! I get it! I can do it!'"

"Yes," I would scribble in the margins, and then I read the passages aloud at the next faculty meeting and quoted them to parents at the next evening meeting.

One of the early challenges that persisted upward of twenty years later was to encourage, reassure, and—presumptuous as it may sound—educate parents about the crucial, profound, and nearly ineffable role the arts play in children's lives. When I first came to St. Augustine's, the school's offerings in the arts ranged from the pallid and conventional to the silly and inappropriate. In most cases, the classroom teachers simply let the children "do art," which was at least relatively harmless but certainly not designed to build sequential skills or stimulate children's imaginations. In the silly category, a music teacher assigned students to memorize the ancient modes (Dorian, Phrygian, etc.) before they had even learned what a scale was.

The biggest obstacle, however, was the parents. To many of them, the arts were a frill, a pleasant diversion perhaps, but a deflection from the real business of the Three Rs. I knew instantly and intuitively that this attitude did a disservice to children. The joys of childhood—inventing games, make-believe, play, storytelling, and fantasy—are as natural to children as breathing. To do anything but give children full and untrammeled encouragement to express these gifts and forces of their inner worlds is not only misinformed but harmful.

At one parent meeting after another, I tried to sell this message in any guise I could muster. Still, parents were apprehensive that time devoted to the arts was time stolen from academics. So I would explain further that the arts enhanced academic performance and that when students learned (for example) to organize sound and rhythms in music, this reinforced their sense of the sounds and rhythms in language. The Orff method of teaching music was a particularly effective way of demonstrating these connections between the arts, education, and happy children.

Yet to some "old guard" parents the very happiness of their children caused suspicion: Was school really supposed to be fun? Were they really learning if they were so happy? At some meetings I found myself defending joy in learning. I came to understand these parents' fears. This "new education" was not what many were used to nor what they had experienced themselves as children. Some bailed out, placing their children in other schools and walking away from their tuition contracts. Fortunately, the majority stayed. Many came to embrace the notion that childhood is a beautiful, precious, and fragile time and came to understand that adult concerns that produce overly disciplined, regimented, and restrictive education are inimical to their children's world.

The best advocates of this message were the children themselves. One of the first graduates of my new school told me recently that when she was in the fifth grade—my first year at the school—she realized something dramatic and special was happening at the school. The changes, she said, were surprising, exhilarating, and, to this day, inspiring. We hired professional artists—teachers who allowed and guided the children's creativity—and the results spoke for themselves. The paintings, assemblies featuring the Orff ensemble, drama productions, and dance concerts were often quite magical. Parents could see their children shine; in fact, the parents themselves were illuminated. These were moments that not only enriched families but sometimes gave everyone a glimpse into the essence of the life force—whether one calls it God, a muse, or the human spirit. Observing these children and the work of a few superb arts teachers, I too acquired a visceral sense of the power and majesty of the arts. I determined to be as fierce a supporter of the arts in the schools as I could be.

Those who questioned our new approaches remained plentiful that year. We began to calculate the deficit we saw looming ahead. I began to feel discouraged. At a personal low point, I came home late after a discouraging day: discipline problems ("See, this new 'openness' doesn't work!"), complaining parents, whining teachers, and threats of more withdrawals of students. One father said he didn't like the inclusion of "them" in "our" school.

I said, "You mean Jews, don't you, Bill?" He simply glared at me.

Just as I sat down to a late dinner, the phone rang. It was a parent who was prominent in the PTA. She thought the school was not quite right for her daughter (actually, the child was doing well), and she was removing her from school. I knew both her and her husband—their parents had been country-club friends of my parents when I was growing up—and they had initially indicated support for my efforts to rebuild the school. However, they just couldn't handle the changes. I hung up the phone and sank into a low-level depression. Was I a fish out of water? Was my philosophy of education simply too "different" for this community?

At first, I answered myself—this isn't a political issue, it's an educational issue. How do children learn best? But I have come to see that there was also a political or social dimension at work here. My desire to foster critical thinking, to make the student body inclusive, even to arrange classroom chairs in a circle rather than rows facing the teacher at the blackboard was not what parents expected. It smelled of change, of a kind of inclusiveness and openness that they may have feared, perhaps consciously but more probably unconsciously. The result of this new educational style might be that their children might question their parents' values; they might choose a different way of life, different social patterns, different political views. Now the school's atmosphere was clearly unusual, not "mainstream," and it was frightening to those who had felt comforted by the status quo. I was depressed by the parents' rejection of my ideas. Nevertheless, I woke up the next morning determined somehow to proceed.

That initial year was difficult for me personally as well. My first marriage was disintegrating. In late spring I went to Frank Grisanti, told him a divorce was in the offing, and said that if he wished, I would resign. He said that he would hear nothing of the sort; everyone had personal problems, and that if I continued to do a good job as headmaster I should stay. I was relieved. Nevertheless, the divorce was painful, and as I look back, I can see that my own immaturity and lack of self-confidence was the primary cause of our dissolution. My former wife, Elizabeth, was and is a wonderful and beautiful woman. I failed her. Fortunately, we have remained friends. In retrospect, the 1970–71 school year was the most chaotic, turbulent, exciting, and transformative year of my life.

During this first year, I set about visiting other established schools to try to acclimate myself quickly to the world of elementary education. Early on, I encountered practices I found utterly bizarre. One school allowed me to observe classes for a morning. I came away disturbed. One incident epitomizes that morning: a child (about five years old) built an unusual structure out of spelling blocks. The teacher wandered by and reprimanded him for using the blocks in a manner for which they were not intended. "These are spelling blocks," she admonished, "not playthings." I was appalled.

Another school discouraged children from reading until they were in second grade (seven years old). "They are not developmentally ready to read until then," the administrator told me. Yet some kids are ready by age four, five, or six. Both schools, I thought, were imposing arbitrary, unnecessary restrictions upon children. The experience of visiting these two schools only strengthened my resolve to try to let the child be the measure of what he or she could achieve rather than imposing a predetermined adult metric. As I was rapidly discovering, children are a mysterious universe unto themselves.

About this time I had been reading *The Inner World of Childhood*, in which Frances Wickes states that adults' unresolved conflicts play themselves out in the lives of the children under their care. As I read this passage for the first time, I sat bolt upright. My God, I thought, parents (and teachers) not only are responsible for knowing what their children are being taught but must also truly know themselves. They must constantly seek to unearth from within their own unconsciousness those unresolved conflicts that—if left unattended—will lead them to make unwise choices that will eventually harm their children.

To further my understanding, I attended several conferences and workshops. One, with Joseph Chilton Pearce (author of *The Crack in the Cosmic Egg* and *Magical Child*), was particularly memorable. Pearce related a study, conducted at a major university, of the "best and the brightest"—young undergraduates who had been class presidents, A students, leaders of activities—all well-behaved and motivated. The study examined their childhoods. "What," Pearce asked us, "do you suppose they all had in common?" Most of us there were educators. We all raised our hands and volunteered our best guesses. We were all wrong, he said. The answer was that each of these students had spent long hours of childhood engaged in blank, open-eyed staring into space. We looked puzzled. "Don't you see?" he continued. "They were daydreamers. They had an active fantasy life. They exercised their imaginations." I went away from the workshop inspired. Rhoda and I redoubled our efforts to allow for creativity and imagination in our curriculum.

As we discussed these issues in faculty meetings and parent evenings, it was an exciting, vital time. Most of us had a sense that we were creating something of real value. Maria Montessori writes, "Play is the work of the child." It is a quotation; however, that still makes some adults nervous. Test scores, drills, and homework assignments are measurable and quantifiable, and hence are all comfortable yardsticks. The value of play is less clear. Whenever I quoted e e cummings, who once expressed his conviction that "nothing measurable is worth a good god damn," members of my school community would tremble. But gradually, the "product" I was selling became more acceptable. Parents saw bored and listless children come alive in the new school, and as the years passed, they came to see that their children's academic skills were growing on schedule, yet with the added ingredient of joy.

Happiness, I preached, is not a detriment to learning: it is essential. School should be a place of adventure, gaiety, mystery. It should be a place of such diversity and constant surprise that everyone can find something that he or she can enjoy and do well. At least some of the time it should even have a zany, carnival-like atmosphere.

As I rethought every previous bedrock value of St. Augustine's, I was forced to rethink the administration of discipline as well. It seemed to me that methods of keeping high-spirited, "unruly" children in line should fit with the other areas of my philosophy: don't be rigid, punitive, and draconian. I sought new ways to approach the problem of keeping order. One challenge was Bobby, a sixth-grade student who drove everyone slightly nuts. Hyperactive, goofy, and sometimes uncontrollable, he constantly disrupted class activities and was frequently sent to my office. Always contrite and always promising to behave better, he would nevertheless soon be sent back to my office. Once, I improvised a different approach. I asked him what he liked to do most. "Play soccer," he responded.

"Tell me about the game," I said. His face lit up, and he enthusiastically began talking about it. I let him get warmed up, but then I interrupted him in mid-sentence to make a quick phone call. I hung up and nodded, and he resumed, but then I yelled for my secretary to give her a quick memo. I nodded, he resumed, then I knocked my books off my desk onto his foot, and so on. Every time he tried to speak, I disrupted him. Finally, he paused, looked at me, and a smile began to form: he got it. We smiled at each other. About twenty years later, I bumped into Bobby in a restaurant. I hadn't seen him since his graduation from sixth grade. He brought me up to date on college, job, etc., then said, "You know, I never forgot that meeting in your office—it really helped turn me around." You lose some, and then you win some.

Given the turmoil, the angry parents who felt betrayed by this young upstart headmaster, and the churchgoing parents of St. Augustine who were upset about the secular humanism that seemed to be pervading the school, I decided to try to mollify feelings by providing a gift to the parent body—a beautiful yearbook. I had been collecting photos all year, and several teachers and parents helped put it together.

Two days before the end of the year, the boxes of yearbooks arrived. Eagerly, I opened one box and took out a copy. The title page read: "St. Augustine's by-the-Sea ESPICOPAL School." I put it back in the box and sent them all back to the publisher. Yes, win some, lose some. In retrospect, I, and I hope the St. Augustine's community, won far more than we lost.

CHAPTER 2

Founding Crossroads:
Birth Pangs and Infancies

I shall be telling this with a sigh
Somewhere ages and ages hence:
Two roads diverged in a wood, and I—
I took the one less traveled by,
And that has made all the difference.

—Robert Frost, "The Road Not Taken"

DURING THE FALL OF THAT first year, a group of parents of sixth-graders came to Rhoda and me and said, "We love the changes and the school you two are bringing into being, but where can we go with our children for next year?"

Rhoda and I looked at each other and said, "We'll get back to you—we have an idea." So we said to each other in private, "Well, here's our opportunity—why don't we start a new middle school and use our sixth grade here as the nucleus for the enrollment?" We decided to hold a "by-invitation" meeting for interested parents at the home of Rhoda and Dwight Makoff. On November 16, 1970, about thirty parents showed up. We outlined our idea and heard their suggestions, and from this meeting, as well as a few more small gatherings, Rhoda and I chose six others to join us in forming a Board of Trustees: J.M. (Mel) Edelstein, Ed Kaufman, Linda Elstad, Gerry Sherman, Peter Swerling, and Barry Rubens. We began meeting regularly.

At one meeting (on December 8, 1970), a discussion of Robert Frost's poem "The Road Not Taken" led to the selection of the name "Crossroads" for the new school, after we had rejected dozens of others, including such ambitious extremes as "Summerhill West" or even "Oxford West." Also, we agreed each of us would donate a founder's fee, and we devised a list of possible locations, presented the second of many budgets, outlined a prospectus, and set a general meeting in January 1971 to announce firmer plans and begin the recruitment drive for students. The board determined to open Crossroads School in September of 1971 with a seventh and eighth grade and for a total enrollment of thirty-two students. Ed Kaufman, a prominent Los Angeles lawyer, provided the school with legal counsel and helped it secure its nonprofit corporate status. At the March Board of Trustees meeting, Rhoda was elected as the school's first director. The board and I determined that I should stay on at St. Augustine's, which had by no means become a smoothly running operation yet. I would also act as the chair of the Education Committee for Crossroads to help Rhoda design the curriculum and hire a faculty.

To hire a Crossroads faculty, we ran ads in various magazines announcing that a new "innovative-traditional" school would open the next fall. One ad in the Saturday Review generated more than a hundred responses. We ultimately hired two "all-purpose" teachers: John Nordquist would teach history, French, and science, and Arthur Tullar would teach English, Spanish, and math. Both—John in particular—were also skilled construction workers. In their spare time, as needs arose, they helped remodel classrooms.

Before John and Arthur were hired, Rhoda and I set out to recruit thirty-two students for September of 1971. Together, we designed a brochure ourselves and used it as our chief promotional piece. As I look back on it now, I am pleased and rather proud to see that it essentially embraces all "seven kinds of intelligence" that Howard Gardner would later identify, establishing his prominent reputation. Our brochure acknowledged the equal importance of linguistic skills, math, physical development, music, visual and spatial awareness, self-understanding, and awareness of oneself in the community. These seven, with the environmental piece coming a little later, have formed the bedrock of all the schools I have tried to create and help develop.

We held coffees, teas, open houses, dinners, and endless meetings to convince prospective families that they should entrust their child to a school that—until late March—had no campus and no faculty. It was a hard sell, but gradually people began signing up. Finally, in late August, we signed up the thirty-second student. Rhoda and I hugged each other and exclaimed, "Well, by God, we've got a school!"

Crossroads School opened its doors in the fall of 1971, housed at a Baptist church in Santa Monica (we used its Sunday school classrooms), and Rhoda greeted a student body of thirty-two seventh- and eighth-graders. The new school was a child of the 1960s, replete with students clad in the quasi-Renaissance dress of the day, an informal atmosphere, and a "progressive" curriculum. It was emphatically, however, not a flaky place academically: 100 percent of the first graduating classes (1976 and 1977) went off to colleges such as Princeton, Mount Holyoke, UC Berkeley, and Reed and reported that they were prepared well for the demands of college.

Rhoda as director and I as educational consultant applied many of our St. Augustine's curricular ideas to the seventh and eighth grades at Crossroads. We offered a variety of arts electives, including a rather haphazard musical jug band (taught by Mary Ann), folk dance, filmmaking, drama productions, weaving, pottery, and printmaking. There were also various "theme days" selected by the students, such as Colonial Day to supplement an American history class and Crazy Day when everyone dressed in outlandish outfits. It was a rich blend of work and play.

Still, these early years—particularly given the distance of time—were for the students a "golden age." Faculty, parents, and students had come together to invent a school; however, each day and each week presented an urgent new problem to be solved. Furthermore, sharing space with a "conservative" church was a challenge in itself. Our kids dressed "messy" and, to be sure, could be quite messy. We had to take everything down on Friday afternoons and make the rooms look brand-new for the Baptist Sunday school, which drove Rhoda nuts. In spite of the church, the students enjoyed the weekly town-hall meetings with Rhoda and had a sense of participating in the building of "their" school. Rhoda however informed me that we needed to find a new campus, or else. After a quick search, we found a building for lease at 1714 21st Street, just three doors south of Olympic Boulevard. The building had formerly been a Motherhood Maternity warehouse, but we created offices and divided the space into classrooms, and in 1972–73 Crossroads found its new home. The back of the building faced an alley that, in time, would become the famous "Alley of Crossroads."

At St. Augustine's we had hit upon an idea that we have used ever since. Rather than hire arts teachers for whom the teaching of art was a primary focus, Rhoda and I hired practicing professional artists who were also good teachers. We believed that artists would carry greater authority and would know how to teach "from the inside out," which would bring an added dimension of experience to their teaching. In addition, the professional artists, usually part-time because of their art careers, generously contributed their talents to the school in a variety of ways: performing, fundraising, decorating the campus, demonstrating career options, and so forth.

In addition to academics and the arts, we built community service into the curriculum from the very beginning. Some students tutored children at a local elementary school, some volunteered at a Head Start center, and some visited local senior citizens' homes. Several students continued to visit and write their "older friends" long after graduation from Crossroads.

The new school also continued the elementary school's policy of not giving letter grades until the ninth grade, of using the greater community as a classroom, and of designing individualized programs—"contracts" as we then called them—for each student. Small was beautiful, and it enabled programs to flourish that would inevitably have to be refined as the school grew larger. In some ways, it truly was a "golden age."

Many of our golden-age policies have become an inseparable part of the school's identity. For example, the founding Board of Trustees determined that ten percent of the operating budget should be applied to financial aid. This money is income that the school receives from tuition-paying families but that is given away in the form of aid. This policy has enabled Crossroads over the years to develop a diverse student population in both race and socioeconomic class.

When my second year at St. Augustine's began, I was officially a bachelor again. It's likely that during this time my attention was not as focused on school issues as it might otherwise have been. My office was adjacent to a faculty work table, and one October day in 1971 I looked up to see Mary Ann Erman, the music teacher, grading some papers. After staring at her for a while, I realized I was tingling like a junior high school boy in the throes of his first crush. We had known each other for over a year now, and I had always considered her beautiful and dynamic. I had surprised myself and her as well by writing her a letter from Salzburg the previous summer, so she was probably (unconsciously) a gleam in my eye even then. But this autumn day was radically different. I made some small talk and managed to arrange a joint visit to an art show that weekend. It wasn't exactly set up as a date, but I clearly thought of it that way. At the end of our visit to the art show, I invited her on an official date. That would be difficult, she said, as she was sort of engaged to another guy. I persisted, and we had our first date on Halloween.

On this date we went to a restaurant called the Cheese and the Olive and walked, hand in hand, back to my tiny rented house a few blocks away where we listened to piano music by two of our favorite pianists, William Kapell and Dinu Lipatti, and talked until midnight. By then I had summoned up my courage for a first kiss. By the end of the evening, I knew I wanted to marry her; it was that clear. We were married on February 19, 1972, and I moved into her house to join two new daughters, Julie, eleven, and Liesl, twelve, who were remarkably sweet and welcoming to this stranger abruptly moving into their lives. In a year and a half, a third child joined us and forever changed my life, both as a man and as an educator.

Married in Malibu
June 16, 1972

That was then, and now, still in 2015, forty-three years later, Mary Ann is still a wild woman whose energy and spontaneous passion for whatever she is doing astounds all who know her. Though she is equally lovely in quiet contemplative moments, her beauty is heightened by the vitality of her inner world. Her music classes and her piano teaching remain as amazing as any teaching I have ever seen.

CHAPTER 3

Headmaster of Two Schools

. . . to fresh Woods, and Pastures new.

—John Milton, "Lycidas"

DURING THE FIRST THREE YEARS of Crossroads, Rhoda Makoff headed the Crossroads middle school and emerging high school, while I headed the elementary school at St. Augustine's. Of course, Rhoda and I spoke almost every day, and we co-designed the high school curriculum, but I had my hands full creating a new culture and new programs at the K–6 school.

After three years of running Crossroads, Rhoda wanted to move on and to return to her roots as a researcher and biochemist. She loved teaching but didn't love administering. In particular, she did not enjoy dealing with demanding, entitled parents. So she announced that 1973–74 would be her final year. Consequently, Rhoda and I wrote some ads and began looking for her replacement.

At my home one Saturday morning, Rhoda and I were discussing possible replacements when we were joined by a neighborhood board member, Irene Jerison, whose daughter, Elizabeth, attended Crossroads. Irene listened for a while and then said, "This is crazy; you, Paul, should run Crossroads—it was your dream, it's your baby!"

After many discussions and meetings it was determined by both the boards of St. Augustine's and Crossroads that I should head both schools since they were really a K–12 entity. Nevertheless, they were two separate schools, on two campuses, with two boards of trustees, and two sets of faculty, parents, and students!

Thus, in the 1974–75 school year I found myself heading a K–5 school on one campus and a seventh-to-eleventh-grade separate school on another campus. Also, during this period we redefined the elementary years to be K-5 and the middle school to be 6-7-8. We did this to align ourselves with the public schools, which were now K-5 and 6-8. The following year we graduated our first senior class in a ceremony that was quite exciting for all of us. The ceremony was held in the backyard of the family whose daughter, Nancy Grinstein, had been the first brave student to sign a contract to attend Crossroads School. Crossroads, it seemed, was here to stay.

Life was further complicated by the need to accommodate the Episcopal roots of St. Augustine's with the changes in culture and enrollment of Crossroads. It was, in fact, no longer a church day school: few students' families were parishioners, many families were Jewish, and most families were there because of the school's progressive curriculum rather than its religious affiliation. I became somewhat of a contortionist trying to appease some folks with humanistic chapels while trying equally hard to alleviate concerns among other parents that the school was leaning too hard on "the Jesus thing."

Finally, the rector, Fred Fenton, an extraordinarily ecumenical, enlightened, and brilliant man, came to me and said, "Look, Paul, let's stop the fiction of St. Augustine being an Episcopal school—it no longer is." He continued, "You are a fine educator. The school is doing God's work, so why don't you just incorporate separately from the church and remain as tenants?" This also seemed to dictate a merger of the two schools.

So in 1982, Crossroads, having completed its first decade, became one K–12 school with two campuses: the St. Augustine Campus and the 21st Street Campus, and we merged the two boards into one. Now, thank goodness, I had one school to run and one board to serve. It brought clarity and greater efficiency to the whole enterprise. The consolidation also gave me some breathing space to reflect on where the school had been and where it might go. Initially, I was enormously insecure about my role as an educational leader. I attended meetings of other local headmasters who, on occasion, treated me with thinly veiled condescension. In a world of traditional, elitist private schools, I was regarded as a bit of a "hippie-artsy" guy presiding over a less than substantial school. I came away from these meetings doubting myself, and after one particular encounter with the heads of the most prestigious schools, I expressed my depression to Mary Ann. She, of course, would hear none of it, told me her opinion of the other elitist schools, and lovingly told me how superior my vision was to theirs. It helped.

I gradually came to see that most people are a little afraid to go after what they know is right; convention and "the way it's always been" weighs them down. However, I believe that the well-being of children and young people requires that their leaders have the courage to take risks or, in some cases, simply to implement best practices.

What made Crossroads different then, and now, I believe, is that we focused upon the individual needs of students. If a student was struggling with the five solids (English, history, math, science, foreign languages), then we would cut him or her back. The curriculum, I would have to argue—even with my own administrators and teachers from time to time—should not be a Procrustean bed to lop off a student's hands or feet to fit the requirements.

As the school's enrollment grew, the space challenges increased, but fortunately so did my opportunities to expand the curriculum and try new programs. Today, people sometimes ask me whether I always had a vision of where the school would go, and, of course, the answer is "no." Often I was just trying to get from Monday to Tuesday. But I did know that providing students the time and space to grow and to discover their interests and passions, along with the encouragement to be themselves, must be at the center of everything we did—no matter what the counter pressures might be. I suppose this has always been a bit of a crusade for me, in part because in my own case learning came slowly, rather late, and only after struggling and hard work. Crossroads in those early years was, I believe, helping to define what is meant by progressive education.

Looking back, it's amazing to realize that from the first class of thirty-two students at Crossroads, whose tuition was $1,500, the school has grown to a combined student body of 1,144, whose tuition is $29,159 for elementary and $34,969 for the middle and upper schools (September of 2014). We still nursed illusions of someday moving from 21st Street to a campus with acreage, babbling brooks, playing fields, trees, and the like. However, whenever such a remote possibility presented itself, we were always several days late and several dollars short. So, instead, we kept expanding up and down both sides of the alley between 20th and 21st streets. Each new acquisition or lease of a new building presented new, and sometimes bizarre, adventures.

CHAPTER 4

The Alley:
Acquiring a Campus

My ambition is to be able to afford to
spend what I'm spending.

—Henny Youngman

THE LOS ANGELES TIMES ONCE referred to the Crossroads campus as having "all the ambiance of a tire factory." Comments such as this were a source of a sort of reverse pride we all felt. Initially, I found myself apologizing for our campus, but gradually I changed my tune. I suppose some might say that you rationalize as you need to, but nevertheless I came to see the funkiness of the campus as an asset. It was at once a great equalizer: a topic for humorous self-deprecation and a place where teenagers felt comfortable, free from pretension and adult concerns of propriety.

In fact, the students themselves were mostly responsible for my change in attitude toward "our alley-centered" school: they took genuine pride in being different from other idyllic, manicured, elegant private schools. During the early years of Crossroads, our senior graduations took place in people's backyards, at the Riviera Country Club, and at the Santa Monica College amphitheater, but in 1980-81, the seniors said "No más. We want to graduate on our own campus." So, aided by a song—an anthem to the alley, written by faculty member David Colloff, we held the 1981 graduation on campus and senior Alexa Junge delivered an inspiring speech, "An Ode to the Alley."

The campus location was pretty much like any industrial area of Santa Monica with warehouses, office buildings, scattered residences, and shops. We didn't begin with a master plan. Instead, little by little, we put together a patchwork quilt of owned and leased buildings. Each building was a sort of adventure, though some were more difficult than others.

Occupying our first building in 1972—Motherhood Maternity Clothes Warehouse—involved a relatively simple lease with options (helped by a student's parent in the company that owned the building), and in time we were able to buy it. The same process transpired with several other buildings. But some buildings were quite problematic. For example, the building on the corner of 21st and Olympic was offered to us initially for fifteen dollars a square foot, which the board approved. Then the owner changed his mind and said, "No, it must be twenty dollars a foot." We convened a special board meeting, and I received reluctant board approval. The owner then raised his price to twenty-four dollars a foot. The board was angry and conflicted, but I finally secured board approval again. Of course, the price now seems like a ridiculous bargain.

One building was a large, well-worn single-story warehouse with a very leaky roof, referred to as the Lichter Building after its owner's name. Since we hoped to tear it down soon, we tried to live with it as it was. Mary Ann taught music in one of the rooms. She put up with the chill and the leaky roof but was not at all happy with the rats scurrying across her classroom. Fortunately, the Lichter Building was torn down in 1989, and in 1990 we constructed a beautiful 15,000-square-foot building designed by the architectural firm of Moore Ruble Yudell and named it the Peter Boxenbaum Arts Education Center. The building was named after the son of our board member Chuck Boxenbaum, a great friend and teacher of mine. Peter had died during his senior year, and Chuck led the fundraising drive for the building. The lead architect was Buzz Yudell, who conceived the building as an "internal plaza and street that celebrate the daily interaction of the students and the arts."

As the building was being constructed, this central plaza was filled with two-story-high scaffolding that obscured how the structure would reveal itself. The day the scaffolding was removed, I was stunned. I entered the building, and it quite literally took my breath away. Buzz had created a stunningly gorgeous space with natural light filtering in—it was to me a temple for the arts. The senior class, however, was contrarily impressed; they thought it was too beautiful for Crossroads.

The beauty of the building gave me an idea: why not try to create in our alley-centered school an "architectural village" with additional buildings designed also by major architects?

The next such project would have a nice surprise. Nestled among the buildings up and down the alley was Lance Haselrig's classic auto body shop. Students crossing the alley from one classroom to another had to be on the alert for cars being towed in. Finally in 1996 we hired architect Steven Ehrlich to design a 10,500-square-foot library and classroom building. I approached a friend and donor, Laura Donnelly, whose family was in the publishing business. I suggested a large donation number that, I told her, would put her family name on the library. She thought about it and ultimately said, "Okay, if I make this donation, I get to name the building?"

"Absolutely," I replied.

"Well then," she said, "I want to call it the Paul Cummins Library." Needless to say, though somewhat humbly, I agreed.

The library building, like Buzz Yudell's Peter Boxenbaum Arts Center, is a dramatically beautiful structure and has won several architectural awards. Steven Ehrlich said of the durable quality of the concrete-like material, "It has an ageless quality, and I appreciate its texture and scale." At night the building sparkles like a jewel. In addition to the usual functions of a library, the building houses a special collections room—the Herbert Zipper Room—which contains books, manuscripts, correspondence, photos, tapes, and CDs all about Herbert's life and times.

Around the time these two stylistically different buildings were being constructed, I began to think of ways we might unify the campus. One world-famous architect suggested we paint the whole campus plaid. He later suggested bus yellow. Neither seemed a very good idea. But, I thought, what about tying the campus together with a large sculpture? Roger and I mentioned the idea to Michael Pestel, an art teacher at Crossroads, and he came up with the Sine Wave to run across the roofs of the two buildings. An alumnus of the school, sportswriter J.A. Adande offers his memory of the *Sine Wave*:

> I can remember when it was still new, still controversial. Sure, it represented an artistic interpretation of a mathematic equation, but it also was an indication of a school still in transition, a place unafraid to do things differently and stand out. And boy did that thing stand out. Somehow it seemed more jarring then, in its natural wood color, than in its current red incarnation. It was such an odd thing to stick on the roof of a school building.

The *Sine Wave* has become a fixture on the campus. We were also able to give the campus a bit of a face-lift by having the overhead telephone wires removed. The city assumed some of the costs, and a major, rather conservative donor contributed a chunk because, as he said, he was embarrassed to send his daughter to such an ugly school.

Not all of the acquisitions of buildings were as easy as the first few. One building—a five-unit apartment building—presented some unique challenges. When we first approached the owner, a rather fiery Argentine, he set a very high price. We said we would meet the price, but he would have to deliver it to us with the rent-control restrictions removed so that we could use it for school purposes. The City of Santa Monica said, "No way." So, no deal.

A few years later, the owner then decided he needed more parking, and so one weekend one of the ground-level rent-controlled apartments was razed. The city threatened to sue. We believed our chances of ever getting the building were slim. He countersued the city, then one night the whole now four-unit building mysteriously caught on fire. The Santa Monica fire chief was quoted as saying it appeared to be arson. The fire was put out, but the apartments were an unusable mess.

Aha, we thought, let's offer a lowball purchase price and take our chances. We offered something like $250,000. What we didn't know was that the city wanted to get rid of pending lawsuits, so they offered to remove the rent control if the owner dropped his suit.

He then contacted us and said, "You can have the building for $450,000" and threatened that otherwise he would lease it to an auto-repair company. This would have meant two auto repair shops in "our alley." We swallowed our pride and paid his price. Win some, lose some. Nevertheless, the $450,000 now also seems like a great deal. So in the long run, I suppose, we really won.

So it went, year after year, fitting together our patchwork quilt of seventeen owned and leased buildings as well as two large buildings on the elementary campus. It was a rather unusual way to create a campus, but it seemed to fit the nature and spirit of the school. Most importantly, it worked.

By 2014 Crossroads was able to purchase fifteen of the seventeen buildings it now occupies.

CHAPTER 5

The Growth of Crossroads:
Some Discoveries

*Ives's "unanswered question" has an answer. I'm no
longer quite sure what the question is, but I do know
that the answer is yes.*

—Leonard Bernstein,
The Unanswered Question: Six Talks at Harvard

EVERYBODY WORKS HARD—AT LEAST MOST people believe they do. When I was
asked, "Isn't being a headmaster hard?" I would say, "I suppose so, but so is selling
shoes, working a cash register, repairing roofs, or performing surgeries."

"Yes, but at least talk about what *is* peculiarly difficult about running a school."
"All right," I would answer, "but only if you understand I'm not complaining or
claiming any special status over any other kind of work."

What I found most difficult about being a headmaster was that it was virtually
a round-the-clock job. Particularly in the early years of the school when days began
at 7:30 a.m. and ended at 6:00 p.m., then the endless evenings of meetings began:
night after night. Often I would come home at 6:00 p.m., take a shower and change
clothes, glance at the mail, wolf down a meal, and drive off to a Board of Trustees

and/or board committee meeting, or parent meeting, or a student art show, drama production, athletic event . . .

Board meetings were productive and supportive. I believe the early board realized we were engaged in creating a new and in some ways groundbreaking organization where people were generous with their time, dollars, and creative thinking. Rarely was there any real dissention or crankiness. Once, when things did get a little tense at a meeting, one board member, Walt Brackelmanns—a psychiatrist—signaled with his hands and got everyone's attention, and then inquired: "What do you get when you cross a donkey with an onion?"

Everyone was rather startled at this unexpected question. Walt continued: "Well, usually you get a donkey with bad breath."

"Sometimes," he continued, "you get an onion with long ears."

"But," dramatic pause, "but, on rare occasions, you get a piece of ass so good it brings tears to your eyes."

We all burst out laughing, and the tension was gone.

In addition to all the official board and parent meetings, there were open houses at each grade level, back-to-school nights, admissions open houses, parent education evenings, and, of course, a host of student events—basketball and volleyball games, art exhibitions, orchestra concerts, chamber music ensembles, choral performances, solo recitals, and four or five drama productions. The headmaster was expected to be present, enthusiastic, and affirmative at all of these events. Often I was expected to speak—to be articulate and even inspiring. I found at times that I yearned for privacy and quiet—just to read, nap, relax, and rekindle my inner fires. I did learn, however, to sleep at night and not stay awake gnashing my teeth over this and that; I learned to prepare speeches and say them aloud while driving to the next event. I learned the value of mentors, as well as the value of attending conferences to stay energized and focused on what is truly essential and current in education.

Most importantly, I found joy in and sustenance from my two little girls, and I spent every minute I could steal from school being with them. Taking them to the library on Saturday mornings, reading to them at night before putting them to bed, or playing catch or kick-the-can with them and their neighborhood friends reminded me every day of why I was in education.

I learned something else at the seemingly endless round of evening meetings: our parents hungered for education and reassurance themselves. Many of them came to these meetings not only because they wanted to be reassured that our school's approach to learning was truly appropriate for their child but to learn how to be better parents. I found that not only did I have to "sell" parents during the admissions process, but I had to continue to sell the Crossroads philosophy of education—our unique balance of academics and the arts, our respect for creativity and the imagination, and our commitment to diversity. Mostly, I had to convince parents to relax and trust that their children would eventually absorb their love and many of their values, even though periods of rebellion, sullenness, isolation, and seemingly self-destructive experimentation were almost inevitable and probably even necessary for growth and eventual independence. They seemed reassured to hear me say this but also seemed to want to hear it again and again. Now that I had children myself, I understood; I may even have repeated this message as often as I did just to convince myself of its fundamental wisdom as well.

Michele Hickey—
my soul mate

Parents had a strong desire to be included in the community we were creating. At first we had offered only a fairly standard version of the PTA, which we called the Parent Association, whose rather vague mission was to carry out activities supporting the school. Then, in 1985, a "blizzard of one" named Michele Hickey (whom a few years later, Crossroads hired as director of development) was elected president of the Parent Association and in only two years transformed the organization into the uniquely dynamic group it is today. A questionnaire was sent to parents during the summer before the start of the school year asking them about their skills and interests and describing in detail the myriad avenues available for parental involvement. Scores of parents took time out from their busy schedules to become involved in the great variety of activities supporting the school. By so doing they made themselves indispensable contributing members of our educational community. I should add that during her years at Crossroads, Michele became my confidante, advisor, and close friend. Her wild sense of humor and her understanding of both the absurdity and beauty of life were among the blessings of my life. She died of cancer in 2005, and I have missed her deeply ever since.

Sometimes parental volunteering had a special quality. In 1987–88 the drama department put on a production of *The Miracle Worker*. After the performances, two parents met with the two student leads to offer their observations and encouragement. They were Patty Duke and Anne Bancroft, the Oscar-and-Tony-winning actresses who had originated the roles of Helen Keller and Annie Sullivan on stage and screen. That evening they were first and foremost Crossroads parent volunteers.

It was difficult not to feel a certain pride in having our high school production validated by magnificent actors. Their presence and support also validated a belief I hold, a belief affirmed years later by my mentor, Herbert Zipper, that only the best is fit for children and youth. Sloppy, mediocre, poorly prepared classes, productions, and programs drive me crazy—not just because I find myself personally embarrassed being associated with such, but because it is damaging to the students to give them a paltry or compromising view of what is possible. Quality is not only possible, it is exhilarating.

We also found that committed, involved parents functioned effectively as ambassadors to other parents. At one orientation meeting for the parents of new seventh-graders, the Parent Association president gave a speech touting the joys of parental volunteering at the school, ending with the ringing declaration "because Crossroads is not just a school; it's a community."

At the reception that followed the formal speeches, the mother of a new student approached the president and said, "After you talked, I nudged my husband and whispered, 'We've come to the right place.'" Another parent told me years later that she once heard me speak and that my philosophy of education moved her to tears, but what really sold her was my shabby sport coat and slacks. She thought that any head of school with so little concern for his appearance must be (although her logic is a little weak) a good educator. Gradually, Mary Ann took over monitoring my clothes.

Meetings led to some groundbreaking innovations. For instance, at the elementary school, as we wrestled with designing a Friday morning chapel service that would be acceptable to parents of all faiths, we formed an "ecumenical committee," and with the immense help of a new rector, Fred Fenton, we designed a format that has worked for more than twenty-seven years! The goal was to celebrate life. The format was as follows:

- Begin in quiet, with the lighting of candles (Father Fenton reminded us of Maria Montessori's observation that one finds two things in all services: candles and music), in particular, a seven-branched candlestick (a menorah), which is common to both the Judaic and Christian traditions.
- Have different classes, groups, and individuals make brief presentations of a life-celebrating nature: a dance, a song, or a story.
- Focus on storytelling.
- Honor specific celebrations and secular rituals—such as Passover, Easter, spring, Christmas, Hanukkah, Yom Kippur, and Martin Luther King Day.
- Close the service with an ancient prayer that is both Christian and Jewish:

> May the words of my mouth
> And the meditations of my heart
> Be acceptable to you, Oh Lord,
> My rock and my redeemer.

Friday chapels were so meaningful that many parents came every Friday whether their child's class was making a presentation or not. We all need ritual and ceremony in our lives. Chapels produced unexpected benefits. Often, when a whole class made a presentation—reading poems, telling stories, or expressing thanks—each child would step up to the microphone at the lectern and say his or her part. By sixth-grade (and later fifth-grade) graduations, we discovered that our children were not nervous speaking in front of audiences. Consequently, in our early graduation ceremonies we provided space in the program for each graduate to say a few words—which they did, often amazing their parents with their poise.

Friday chapels and our unique graduations (in many ways an expansion of the chapel format) also led to the discovery of how to structure memorial and funeral services. When I became a headmaster for the first time, I took the job with unrestrained enthusiasm and optimism; it never occurred to me that I would have to deal with death. Yet, from the time I became headmaster in 1970 until 1994, there were thirty-one deaths of school-related people—teachers, parents, and, alas, eighteen students and alumni. I was often called upon to speak and, in several cases, to organize and preside over the entire service. While I learned several things from these experiences, the primary lesson was to blend ceremony with intimacy—to seek an authentic and engaging experience for everyone. The way to honor each deceased person, I concluded, was to bring as much of his or her essence to the service as we could, through music, readings, anecdotes, and witnesses. We provided a structure, which consisted of a beginning (lighting of candles and music, usually chosen by the parent or loved ones); a middle with heartfelt testimonials, stories, often witty and humorous, always with a personal dimension; and an end (a closing prayer and appropriate student-centered music). Often I would speak first and try to put the tragedy into some larger perspective. Also, we always provided wonderful memorial programs for people to take home with them, giving them a sense of having something to "keep." The programs often included photographs, a poem, a piece of writing by the family or by the deceased—simple but appropriate. These services almost always seemed to help not just the family, but the entire community—for they were not just tragic terminal moments, but true celebrations.

At several funeral services, I found words from the conclusion of Thornton Wilder's *The Bridge of San Luis Rey* as a helpful means of suggesting the crossing of boundaries between those alive and those for whom we grieve:

> There is a land of the living and a land
> of the dead and the bridge is love, the only
> meaning, the only survival.

These were the words I used to close the service of a much-beloved teacher at Crossroads whose life and death journey offered another remarkable moment in the school's coming of age.

Steve Morgan was hired in 1973 as the third teacher at Crossroads. First an English teacher, he was immediately a favorite among students. He was kind, gentle, and handsome, and he possessed a zany sense of humor; to know him was to love him. We became fast friends. He progressed from English teacher to director of the middle school to director of admissions. Parents loved him as much as the students did. He became an institution within the institution. A bravura performance by Steve was the centerpiece of each fall's admissions open house for families we hoped would choose Crossroads for their incoming seventh-grader next year. As prospective families sat in a large assembly room, the current year's ninety or so seventh-graders ran in one by one and took seats in the front row, as Steve rapidly called out each one's name. I can only imagine the wonderment and delight in the minds of future Crossroads parents as they saw the director of admissions knowing each (comparatively new) seventh-grader well enough to call him or her by name.

On one occasion, Steve, as admissions director, was interviewing a mother and father who were considering the school. Steve sat in his chair with one leg folded under him, and unbeknownst to him, his foot had fallen asleep. When the interview concluded, everyone stood up, but when Steve put his weight on the one foot, he collapsed upon the mother and they both fell on the floor with Steve on top. He looked up at the stunned husband and with a sheepish half-smile pointed down to his shoe and said, "Foot fell asleep." Surprisingly, the family enrolled their daughter.

One day in the fall of 1986, Steve came to see me. He had been diagnosed as HIV-positive. We looked at each other for a moment, then both of us were flooded with tears. I hardly knew what to say: in those days that diagnosis was a death sentence. Later we turned to practical matters and agreed that he would stay on as director of admissions that school year unless the AIDS manifested itself visibly. Steve finished the year in good health, so we determined to try another year, although we did appoint Tom Nolan as an assistant director of admissions, ostensibly because the workload at Crossroads had grown, but really to learn the ropes in case Steve had to stop work. The 1987–88 school year progressed fairly well for Steve until about April of 1988, when the Kaposi's sarcoma spots that had begun to appear started to become noticeable. We decided it was time to act. I wrote a letter to the entire parent-student-alumni community telling them exactly what was happening. Simultaneously, we gathered faculty and staff together on a Friday afternoon, and Steve told everyone his story. There were few dry eyes in the room. We mailed the letter to the larger community that afternoon. Steve told our school community that he was taking a medical leave to fight the disease, but we all knew he was saying goodbye.

Steve lived a little over one more year, though his final months were painful and difficult. He died on July 19, 1989. But in May of 1989, before school was out, I invited Steve over to school on some pretense, and several of us met him just around the corner of the alley that runs down the middle of our "urban campus." We put Steve in the back seat of a convertible and drove him around the corner and down the alley, which was lined on both sides with the entire student body (more than 600 students), all wildly cheering. It was our version of a New York ticker-tape parade. We drove him up to the middle school classroom building. I said a few words over a loudspeaker, and we unveiled a sign on the building—the Steve Morgan Middle School building. It was an intensely emotional moment—a moment of pride shared by many people. That evening, Steve had a friend drive him back to take a picture of the building with his name on it so he could send it to his mother.

The funeral service was one that few people who attended will ever forget. A year earlier, Steve had told me about a particularly moving funeral he had been to, where a song that he loved had been sung: "I'll Be Seeing You." Did I know it? he asked me. "Yes," I said, "Mary Ann played it on the piano at my father's funeral."

At Steve's funeral, the song was to be sung by a Crossroads graduate, but she developed laryngitis, so I played the piece on the piano by myself. I could barely get through it but managed somehow. The speeches, poems, and music all captured something of Steve's spirit, but words from a letter he had written to the entire school a year earlier were printed in the program, and they summed up who Steve was:

> So I am not leaving, when I do leave, with bitterness. I
> am leaving with sorrow that I could not stay longer. My life
> has been so blessed. I have had the rare, fair treatment of
> loving family, loving friends, and loving associates in my
> work. Everyone has been so kind to me; I wish for everyone
> that life could be this good to them.

As fate would have it, my second encounter with AIDS also began in 1986. During the summer I received a request for a meeting with a woman named Elizabeth Glaser. I will, for a moment, let her tell the story of our first meeting as she recounted it in her book *In the Absence of Angels*:

> We applied to your school, and we have been accepted, and we were planning on having our
> daughter, Ariel, start kindergarten here in September. But I just found out that she, my son,
> and myself are all infected with the AIDS virus.
>
> I started to cry. I was sure he would send me away and tell me to find another school. Paul
> Cummins walked over and put his arms around me. "You are part of our family. We want
> you here." He held me as I cried.
>
> Paul Cummins was the first person we didn't know who reached out to my family with-
> out any hesitation or fear. He said he had been appalled by the stories about children with
> AIDS around the country being mistreated in schools. He was convinced that AIDS was
> not spread by casual contact, and he felt that a child with HIV or AIDS deserved to have as
> normal a life as possible for as long as possible.

As it turned out, Ariel spent very few days at Crossroads as her illness progressed rapidly; she died on August 12, 1988. Those were the early days of AIDS, and there was little being done for children. So, despite her grief, Elizabeth and two friends formed the Elizabeth Glaser Pediatric AIDS Foundation and raised substantial funds and deepened national, public, and governmental consciousness. Elizabeth was a true national hero. She died on December 3, 1994. Suffice to say, I will never forget her. She was one of those people you feel blessed to have known.

Without fully realizing it, I suppose I did borrow a page from the book of my former high school headmaster, who often spoke of schools as "redemptive communities." In the first few years of Crossroads, and in subsequent years as well, I have found the concept intriguing. For example, about the third year of Crossroads, five tenth-grade boys were caught using marijuana on campus. It was truly a crisis: not only could we ill afford the loss of tuition income, we (Rhoda and I) feared even more the damage to our fragile reputation that five expulsions would cause. However, we tried to keep our eyes on the ball, which, we concluded, was what was best for the students. Simply expunging them from the school didn't seem to be in anyone's best interests. We met with the families, with board members, and with our faculty. Finally, Rhoda and I determined to suspend them from school for three weeks, during which time they were required to have at least three family counseling sessions as a ticket for readmission. Two families found this verdict too intrusive, and they did not return. While this may seem ludicrous today, when most private schools would summarily and permanently expel them, at the time our actions seemed demanding. Three families did return, and two of them told us in later years that the counseling sessions were a turning point for the entire family. They were grateful. One boy became student body president of Crossroads in his senior year and later became a full professor of political science at the University of Wisconsin.

Now, cut to almost twenty years later. Same issue. Same grade: a tenth-grade boy caught with marijuana. We expelled him for his entire eleventh-grade year. However, we told him that if he compiled a spotless record elsewhere, he could reapply for his twelfth-grade year. He did both. We accepted him, and at the end of his senior year with us, so did Yale.

People look to the headmaster as a type of judge who always knows what is best to do. They want to believe in an authority and feel the security in believing that someone always knows the fair thing to do. The irony I discovered early on was that people came to me for decisions when I didn't know what the hell to do any more than they did. But I quickly learned that I couldn't let on about this: they needed a decision, and I had to render it. I learned the art of improvisation as well as the art of listening. I found I made my biggest blunders when I acted before thoroughly listening to all parties. It is often hard to remember this truth. Even in my twenty-second year of being a headmaster, I acted hastily on incomplete information in a "drug bust." Consequently, I mismanaged the situation about as badly as I can remember ever having done. I suspended several students and then, when new "evidence" surfaced, I was forced to meet with all the parents involved to rescind my action and apologize. I thought I looked like a fool although several parents told me afterwards they respected my willingness to admit and rectify a mistake.

I learned the importance of enlisting support and garnering "investment" from your own teammates before attempting to implement new plans. Sounds obvious?

Of course. But easy to forget. For example, I once decided it would be good to begin the school year with a faculty retreat at a "New Age" community center in the Ojai mountains. As I envisioned it, we would have quiet time, sit in Council (a discussion format employing a facilitator), and discuss our dreams and visions for the school year. There was only one hitch: I didn't discuss this plan with the faculty in advance. They felt put upon; they felt my "quasi-religious" "hippie-New Age-touchy-feely" values were being imposed on them. Instead, they wanted to be at school fixing up their classrooms. They were angry and in no mood to embrace my idea of a communal gathering to begin the school year. Rebelliously, they soon began leaving the retreat center, and after one or so days of a planned three-day retreat, I found myself alone with my friend and facilitator. It was a semi-disastrous way to begin a school year. It was laughingly referred to in later years as "Paul's Waterloo." I don't know whether the comparison with Napoleon was apt, but I definitely picked up on the lesson that was there to be learned.

Finally, I discovered that bad decisions sometimes result from a failure to give credit to the opposition, a failure to acknowledge the complexity of a given issue and the legitimacy of those who oppose you—even if you sincerely believe that your idea has the greater merit. During the early years of the elementary school, I wanted to get rid of school uniforms, the very notion of which seemed antithetical to the philosophy of the education I was trying to promote. But I didn't want to create another furor among the parents. So I acknowledged at meeting after meeting that while I was not in love with the idea of uniforms, I understood that they prevented competition among kids, kept poorer students from feeling embarrassed about not having "the right" clothes, and made morning decision-making about "what to wear" less stressful for all. I acknowledged these points so often that finally at a Parent Association meeting one parent stood up and said, "Paul, we know you hate the idea of uniforms, so why don't we get rid of them?"

Other parents joined in and said, "Yes, let's get rid of them." They took a vote and in three minutes it was done. If *I* had attacked uniforms, the parents might have resisted. Because the impetus had come from them, it was a simple process.

Mostly, I learned to listen, to try to keep the students' best interests at heart and then to act decisively and with clarity. I found that every time I had listened to all, listened to my own inner wisdom, then tried to act decisively yet gently on behalf of children's needs and welfare, I generally made good decisions.

Recently, a Crossroads graduate asked me how I would describe my style and philosophy of administration. My response is that my style is probably somewhat informal and seemingly casual. One colleague described my approach to decision-making as "ready, fire, aim." Roger Weaver, writing a tribute for the 2002 Cabaret school talent show, said, "Paul generates five good ideas a day and believes in what I call the self-propelling good idea. That is, if you get a good idea, you must launch it, and somehow it propels itself into success." Roger's humor aside, I suppose I do believe in taking risks and not assuming you can map out programs elegantly before implementing them. I do believe that often it is best to simply start and refine as conditions evolve. I know that many of the programs Crossroads still values most were born in just this manner.

In addition, I believe in treating everyone as kindly as possible on the cliché-ish theory that "what goes around comes around," and that kindness is crucial to creating a school culture where everyone feels valued.

Finally, I believe that most people thirst for meaning and purpose, and that the role of the leader is to keep reminding everyone of why we are doing what we do—namely, to help young people discover who they are and to help them find their own sense of meaning and self-worth. Lofty as this may sound, it is, I believe, what makes the whole enterprise of education worthwhile, and most people want to drink from this well. Building a better world is done one person at a time.

Paul Cummins, Rhoda Makoff, Bob Riddle, and Roger Weaver

CHAPTER 6

Mysteries:
An Innovative Idea

When will you cease to worship
and to love the pitcher? When will you
begin to look for the water?

—Rumi

If intelligence is the wisdom to speak,
wisdom is the capacity to listen . . .

—Richard Wrangham & Dale Peterson

SOMETIME DURING THE SPRING OF 1983, a twelfth-grade student walked boldly into my office and said, "May I talk?" Then, without waiting for my invitation, she plopped herself down on my couch and blurted out, "Tomorrow, tomorrow, tomorrow—is that all you adults ever talk about?" She went on to say that all she heard of was preparing for the future—tomorrow's quiz, next month's SATs, the April college acceptance dates, college majors, and choice of vocation—even where she might ultimately settle down, but never about today's dreams and fears and personal complexities. She concluded by saying, "When do we get to enjoy today?" Then, abruptly, she got up and left—feeling, I suppose, slightly better for at least having vented and having been heard.

I pondered her words glumly on my own for several days, then over coffee with my friend and mentor Jack Zimmerman—an extraordinary educational visionary—who said, "Well, why don't you do something about it?" He then explained Council to me.

with fellow Headmasters—
Jack Zimmerman and Nat Reynolds

Council is an ancient practice originating in Native American traditions. It is a practice that Jack had introduced earlier at a school he helped create named Heartlight. The school did not survive for financial reasons, but the practice of Council was a great success. I left our meeting exhilarated: here was a way to address the concerns of the girl who came to see me. Here was a way, I was soon to discover, for dealing directly with adolescent anger and alienation.

Council begins with a circle. Students usually sit on the floor, with an adult facilitator in charge of moving things along. Sometimes the lights may be dimmed and a candle lit in the center of the circle to imbue the process with seriousness and ceremony. The group also selects a "talking piece"—perhaps a gourd, a small stone, or a special wand or rattle—which one must hold to speak. Thus, each person in the circle has a chance to speak, uninterrupted, and each person must listen to others without speaking. The rules of Council are simple:

1. Speak honestly.
2. Listen from the heart.
3. Be concise.

One is also allowed to simply pass the talking piece without speaking; in fact, silence often communicates powerfully. The leader of the given Council stresses the importance of confidentiality: that what is said in Council is sacred and must not be repeated to others outside of Council. In more than twenty-seven years of this program at Crossroads, students have honored this principle with remarkable integrity and loyalty; rarely has a student's trust been violated by another student. I believe that the students are so grateful for the trust we place in them that they wouldn't consider jeopardizing the program by betraying that trust. Council—on any given day—may or may not have a specific theme. Some days students will simply go around the circle giving a "weather report," that is, talking about how they are feeling and dealing with life at that moment. Or a given Council may focus on a topic such as death, divorce, the breakup of friendships, social pressure, or any other theme that may emerge.

Armed with a beginner's understanding of Council, and with Jack Zimmerman's promise to help me launch the program, I decided to waste no time. With Jack as facilitator, we began several Councils of fourteen to sixteen seniors each. We decided right off the bat to give the Council period a special name—"Mysteries"—since this would be much of its subject matter. The adolescent years are times of profound change, confusion, and mystery. Students' bodies are changing as are their feelings toward their parents, friends, and themselves. Their moral compasses fluctuate wildly, and love and hate exist almost simultaneously. Adolescents are starting to form a sense of identity, but it is fragile and insecure, and all of this is happening so fast they have no way of understanding it. When we help them make some sense of it all, it helps not only their inner world but even their academic performance.

When we launched the class, I thought parents would be hostile, teachers would welcome it, and students would resent "yet another program" in their busy lives. I was wrong on all three counts. The parents—almost from day one—loved the program. Their children were coming home and starting discussions about friendship, respect, listening, the complexities of modern life, and so on. When the parent had previously tried to initiate such discussions, their teenage children would clam up, but not so when their children actually initiated the conversation. At first, the faculty was frightened and resistant—partly because they resented the intrusion of a new program in the schedule, and partly because they feared students would "discuss" them in Council circles. The students embraced the program almost from the very beginning; their only complaint was that we had waited until their senior year to provide it.

Despite widespread enthusiasm, a few parents expressed concerns: was this a touchy-feely program? Was it group therapy? Was it an encounter group? Was it a quasi-religious gathering? No, I explained, regarding all four concerns. One, there is no touching at all in Council. Two, because each individual speaks as an individual and because there is no specific response by the leader/facilitator or the group to anyone, no group therapy takes place during Council. It is, I suppose, true that speaking from the heart about one's life is therapeutic, but the group's focus is not problem-solving for any individual. Three, for the same reasons, it is not an encounter group. The facilitator permits neither combativeness nor confrontation. Fourth, there is no dogma or religious content. The only ceremonial ritual is lighting a candle. "The candle," explains Zimmerman, "is seen as asking for guidance and light. It changes the environment; it's like when you start a story with 'Once upon a time.' It shifts consciousness." Once parents heard this explanation, they were reassured.

The Council program, which was launched for seniors in 1983, was such a success that it eventually was added at every grade level. Thus, the whole school now "practices" Council, and by the time students graduate, I believe they have gained listening skills, a greater awareness of others, and a greater sense of self-awareness. I have had college admission officers and interviewers say over and over that they can pick Crossroads students out of any group of high school applicants—they have a certain self-confidence and openness that is not the norm. If knowledge of how to function in community and self-knowledge are two forms of intelligence, then Mysteries is a clear way of developing these two "intelligences" within the curriculum. Many people fail to succeed in life simply because they can't listen to others; they can't work well in a group; they don't perceive how others perceive them; they don't know their own limitations. Mysteries helps young people gain these insights.

The beauty of Council is that it enables all of us involved to go deeper into ourselves and to remind ourselves that whether in family, school, or the workplace, what fuels each of our lives are relationships. For me, whether sitting in Council with teachers, students, or family, the process invariably required me to listen with my heart to what others were saying. This is sometimes called "deep listening." Invariably, the risk is that the process becomes a little emotionally sloppy, engendering discomfort within the group. This is, however, a risk worth taking, for when it truly works, which is more often than not, everyone is enriched. Council has helped many people get through difficult times.

One such time for me occurred in 1990 when a seventh-grade boy, Michael Smith, was killed in traffic walking back to school from his physical education class in the park three blocks down the street. I was devastated. The parents refused to see me. They were both destroyed and angry. I was ready to quit my job—how could I be a school head if parents couldn't have their children return from school alive? My feelings dragged lower and lower and lower. As fate would have it, I was at that time engaged in an all-men's Council-training group at Jack Zimmerman's home. I went to the group shortly after the tragedy, and Jack, seeing my agony, put me in the center of the circle and had each man present address me personally. It was extraordinary. Many told me stories of their own where they felt they had let someone else down; a couple of cases resulted in deaths—one a young brother of the man addressing me. During the course of the evening we were all reduced to tears, and gradually a sense of forgiveness took place, and we all realized the importance of going beyond our pain and reaffirming life. I still, however, can barely speak Michael Smith's name without my eyes stinging. Nevertheless, Council at least helped me get on with my life as an educator.

Since it was established almost thirty years ago, the Mysteries program has not only grown and flourished at Crossroads, it has also spread to other private and public schools. In fact, I believe my role in creating Council at Crossroads and promoting it in the wider community may well be one of my most significant lifetime contributions. The story of bringing Council to Palms Middle School was told by a Los Angeles freelance writer, Kathy Seal, in the Pacific Southwest Airlines magazine *Spirit*:

> The well-respected magnet school, like many others in Los Angeles, has a global admixture of students speaking more than thirty different native languages. This spring, a few typical early adolescent conflicts—taunting remarks, a fistfight—had taken on non-typical racial overtones. Lana Brody, the vice principal, remembers feeling sad and not knowing what to do with her fear.
>
> She was worried about what she saw happening, events that she now realized were preliminaries to the L.A. riots. It was almost an ominous foreboding that you could smell or touch or feel.
>
> Brody wanted some kind of program for Palms that would break down stereotypical thinking among students. "I wanted something that would imbue kids with proper ethics and understanding they'd need to build the bridges that would be necessary in their adult lives in this city," she says.
>
> Cummins and Zimmerman suggested forming a "council" of student-body officers and other student leaders at Palms. For the past ten years, Crossroads and several other private schools in southern California have used such groups as part of a "Mysteries," or human-development program.
>
> One such session last April found Zimmerman sitting cross-legged on a classroom floor in a circle with teacher Sylvia Thomas and ten kids from a variety of ethnic backgrounds, including African, Japanese, Jewish, Mexican, Korean, Filipino, Chinese, Vietnamese, and Arab. A candle burned in the circle's center. It was the evening of the jury decision in the

second Rodney King beating trial, and Zimmerman asked the kids to give a "weather report" on how they'd feel as an L.A. City Council member on this day. One boy was sprawled on the floor, chin cupped in his left palm and elbow on the floor. Another rested his head on his arms, which were folded on the corner of the teacher's desk. A girl on the rug fidgeted with a pencil and picked at her fingernails with a teenager's nervous energy. All listened quietly as each spoke, one by one, of their confusion, tension, and anger.

After Jack Zimmerman's initial success with seniors, along with two other gifted Council leaders, Maureen Murdock and Ruthann Saphier, we added a retreat to the Ojai Foundation as a "rite of passage" ceremony for seniors. The Ojai Foundation has been in existence since 1975 and is a spiritual retreat center north of Santa Barbara. The trip for seniors at the end of their years at school was a profound experience for most of the boys and girls and has remained an essential ingredient in the Crossroads experience.

The three- or four-day retreat includes a series of Councils as well as alone time—sometimes referred to as a vision quest. In these retreats the alone time is one hour the first day, with no pen, paper, or radio, and three hours the next day, with pen and paper allowed. The final day concludes with a sweat lodge modeled after the Native American tradition. Initially, some kids pooh-poohed it as "Indian legend" but most were and continue to be willing to suspend judgment and go with the flow.

For me, the experience of sitting for forty to forty-five minutes in the darkness with fourteen to fifteen seniors sweating profusely and giving themselves over to the process was extraordinary. Time itself seemed to slow down, and the lives of those seniors—their time at Crossroads, what their futures might be, the reality that many for whom I cared deeply I would hardly ever see again—all this worked over me as the sweat performed its magic. A sense of solidarity and love was and continues to be the essence of the retreat.

Postscript

When seniors return from the trip and are seen by others hugging goodbye and laughing and crying, other students now acknowledge them with a knowing nod and say, "Oh, they just returned from Ojai."

Council has become more essential now than when we began it nearly three decades ago. It is a place where the young, in a setting of trust and confidentiality, can express their fears and speak of their hopes and dreams, their verities and truths. Young people today live in times when the fear of nuclear annihilation has expanded into new anxieties—fear of environmental degradation, toxicity, and even extinction; fear of strange new diseases; fear of not finding a job; fear of violence in the streets and neighborhoods; and the vague fears of living meaningless lives in a culture and world whose values are contradictory and confusing.

When students have a time and place to tell their stories, they learn to be more careful in forming snap judgments about others. Often, they sit in Council with students they had written off years ago as "geeks" or "weirdos" or "jerks." But as they listen to each other, they learn that these students have similar fears and rich interior worlds. New friendships are formed. Old pre-judgments (i.e., prejudices) are discarded. Furthermore, boys—who in our macho-saturated culture are *not* encouraged to express emotion—learn in Council to express and to hear feelings. They learn that it is not unmanly to share their inner world with others.

Council can be a place where the many stresses that students experience are shared, discussed, and in some cases alleviated. When faculty members participate in Councils, they come to see the school day and the lives of individual students in a different light. Like all adults who deal with the young, teachers are better talkers than they are listeners. The Mysteries program focuses on listening to the students.

"Why is it a sin to be vulnerable?" a Crossroads senior once asked in Council. The answer I would offer is that being vulnerable, being open to others, and sharing ideas and feelings with kindness and humility is a profound human achievement. As the poet Peter Levitt wrote, "Sin is alienation from the self; it is the distance between wholeness and hollowness." Mysteries classes with their Council format are not some sort of miracle cure, but they do help to counteract the materialism, egotism, racial and class divisiveness, and frantic sense of despair and meaninglessness that our young (and older) people are feeling. Conflict, anger, bigotry, and selfishness are all the result of people living alone with their fears and anxieties and, consequently, living apart from community. Council teaches us how to live *in community*. And year after year when I talk to graduates, invariably they refer to Council as the Crossroads gift that keeps giving in their lives. I tell them—so, too, in my life.

CHAPTER 7

Joy and Mutual Respect:
The Core of Community at Crossroads

It seemed I was a mite of sediment
That waited for the bottom to ferment
So I could catch a bubble in ascent.
I rode up on one till the bubble burst,
And when that left me to sink back reversed
I was no worse off than I was at first.
I'd catch another bubble if I waited.
The thing was to get now and then elated.

—Robert Frost, "In a Glass of Cider"

IN THE EARLY YEARS, AS we were "making it up as we went along," creating traditions and institutions for our fledgling campus, we unwittingly continued to knit together the "soul of the school." We began each school year with an Alley Party with food, games, and entertainment for the entire student and parent body—eventually more than a thousand people simply enjoying hanging out together. There were Originals, evenings of original plays written, directed, and produced by students, and Forum Days, when regular classes were suspended, and the entire school focused on a significant issue. One year it was racism and homophobia; another year it was conflict in the Middle East. Every decision we made only reinforced our core beliefs about the right way to nurture and encourage the development of our students' best potential.

Although we placed a premium value on the arts, it was not only in the arts that creativity flourished. Classroom activities, science fairs, family-tree exhibits, journalistic essays, classics festivals, senior projects ranging from full-length books to slightly bizarre short films, and even student elections provided opportunities for wild expressions of the imagination. Often a student who failed to shine in academics, athletics, or traditional arts classes did so in one of these other activities, surprising him- or herself by discovering new and unsuspected talents. A "virtuous cycle of positive reinforcement" began. These personal surprises helped the student think more positively about him- or herself and consequently perform more effectively elsewhere in school. Often faculty members came to see that student in a new light, as worthy of more respect, which in turn helped the student perform even better. Adolescents can be insecure and overly sensitive and thus difficult for adults to relate to. Yet this same insecurity and sensitivity can also make them wonderfully responsive to encouragement and kindness. At Crossroads we took very seriously e e cummings's declaration that "We do not believe in ourselves until someone reveals that deep inside us something is valuable, worth listening to, worthy of our trust, sacred to our touch. Once we believe in ourselves, we can risk curiosity, wonder, spontaneous delight or any experience that reveals the human spirit." How could this important core value of Crossroads have been phrased any better?

Gradually, I came to an exciting realization that encouragement and affection are the essence of education at its best. I learned that these two qualities make possible real academic challenge and artistic growth, they help athletes and regular students perform better, and they make students look forward to school. Perhaps the greatest achievement of Crossroads and, by extension, of my career as an educator has been the wacky, creative, joyful atmosphere of the place. To this day, I wonder how I could have been responsible for creating such an environment. I am a rather private, quiet, book-loving person. Perhaps this atmosphere just "happened," and I was a fortunate bystander. Or perhaps I can claim some credit for having allowed and encouraged the effervescent creativity of this "alternative school style" to evolve. I know I became increasingly excited by being surrounded by offbeat teachers and students; although they can be a "pain in the administrative ass" sometimes, more often their unpredictability and originality have supplied the school with its juice, its distinct flavor.

I also know that as the school became wackier and more joyful, I became more emboldened to take new risks. Instead of having new ideas subjected to committee review and careful analysis, answering endless concerns of "Why do this?", my responses more often became "Let's try it—it sounds valuable and, most importantly, it sounds fun." Life is so short, I reasoned, let's enjoy it while we have it; let's help students enjoy their youth.

I think also that a growing recognition of my own learning history prompted me to be more flexible and forgiving of student weaknesses, needs, and developmental issues, as well as to recognize the importance of making the curriculum as diverse as possible. Gradually, I came to see that I had been a late bloomer; a slow learner; and an overachiever. I recognized that my IQ (based on every standardized test I had ever taken) was most likely average, that in college it took me longer to learn than many of my quick classmates, and that I didn't start really blossoming as a student until my third year of college. Fortunately, I grew up in the 1950s, when these three attributes were not educationally crippling. Today any one of these three would make life difficult for any student. Today with my SAT scores I would never have gone to Stanford. Consequently, I developed a more patient and supportive attitude toward students who were struggling. "Give them time and encouragement" became my mantra.

I tried to allow as much goofiness as possible, as long as it did not involve threats to life and limb. For a number of years, a faculty-student water balloon fight took place at the end of the year, with much hilarity. Once we rented a snow machine and, on a sunny California day, had a faculty-student snowball fight on the playground. It was rather astounding to see a relatively reserved teacher fire a direct hit on a student athlete or to witness a sweet, seemingly innocent tenth-grade girl nail an upper-school dean. I was pelted several times myself, but my quarterback's arm enabled me to get off a couple of scores myself. Another day, some students organized an outrageous but highly amusing Jell-O-wrestling competition (think mud-wrestling, but sweeter). One time, after a senior boy expressed some uptight homophobic views, five of his friends cross-dressed in flamboyant garb and followed him around all day. This was, however, difficult to explain to a group of Japanese educators in dark three-piece suits who happened to be visiting Crossroads that day.

The alley that runs through the Crossroads campus is the central artery of the school, supplying the school with a major part of its identity. Over the years students have expressed a reverse pride in bragging to their friends from nearby elitist private schools that their school, Crossroads, has an alley in the middle of the campus. Somehow, the alley is the great equalizer: students from $5 million homes five minutes to the north and students from gang- and drug-infested low-income housing five minutes to the south gather each day in the alley, and both pretension and deprivation melt away amid the funky but pleasant atmosphere. Lunchtime in the alley is usually a "happening" replete with dancing or hacky sack. There can be DJs playing music over a loudspeaker, everything from Bill Evans to rap. Sometimes students will set up a podium and put on lunchtime performances. There are lunch trucks, with a Good Food Truck and Junk Food Truck, both equally popular. During Dog Days, faculty and students alike are allowed to bring their dogs to school. The carnival-like atmosphere relieves tension and makes possible the achievement of an enormous amount of academic work without the usual pressure that prep schools impose on their students.

Located in the "elitist Westside" of Los Angeles, Crossroads has attracted many celebrity parents. Some have been rather demanding, a few have felt entitled, but most have been a bonus for the school, and several became good friends. When it came to their children, they were not different from any other loving, sensitive, and worried parents. Through several of our comedic parents, the school and I learned to laugh at ourselves. Perhaps more than anything else, this ability to not take oneself super seriously has earned the respect of the students and parents alike. Without surrendering authority or credibility, I was able to stand in front of both groups on occasion and say, "Sorry, folks, I think I messed up on this or that" or to say, "We have a problem here, and let's try to figure out together what to do."

As Crossroads learned to laugh at itself, we decided to organize and put on a fundraising event known as Cabaret, an evening of song, dance, and comedy combining the talents of faculty, parents, students, and parent celebrities, all performing together.

The stars usually had cameo roles in skits poking fun at the school and the West Los Angeles lifestyle. One skit brought nine adults, all representing one applicant, into the office of the director of admissions: "I'm her natural mother," "I'm the second wife's husband," "I'm the father's third wife," and so on. At the culmination of these introductions, the admissions director says, "And now let's talk about Lisa," whereupon one of the nine parental figures exits, shrieking, "Lisa? LISA? I'm in the wrong meeting!"

At one Cabaret there were technical difficulties, so comedian Norm Crosby was asked to come to the rescue and go out on stage and do some stand-up shtick to stall for a while. He was introduced and stepped out to polite applause, which he received by saying, "Thank you, thank you very much for the ovulation." Ten more minutes of malaprops followed, and the crisis was covered up. On a separate occasion, after I gave an impassioned speech at a parent education evening, Norm came up to me afterward, clasped my shoulders with both hands and said, "That was really adequate!"

During another Cabaret, in 1989, Anne Bancroft was to sing "It Had to Be You," with the lyrics changed so that the *you* she was expressing her love to was

Crossroads School. Sadly, the day before, Anne's dear friend actress Gilda Radner had died, and Anne was distraught. She came out on stage singing and dancing but at first was unable to remember her lines. Her husband, Mel Brooks, was sitting in the first row and immediately picked up on her distress. So Mel quietly fed the lines to Anne, who carried it off so well that few people realized what was happening: *Wow*, I thought to myself, *what a pro!*

Another time I asked Anne to be a keynote speaker at a conference on the arts that I hosted. She gave her talk and, at the end, opened it up for a Q & A. One participant asked, "Miss Bancroft, when did you know you were going to be an actress? Did a high school or college director, or agent, or drama teacher help you to know?" Anne, without a pause, said, "Well, my dear, I'm so damn talented, I've always known." It wasn't arrogant; it was delightful, and we all cheered.

Another wonderfully talented lady, Bea Arthur, called St. Augustine's during the first month of Rhoda's and my first year there. She wanted her two sons admitted. Rhoda told her we were full. To which Bea replied, in her most assertive, deep voice, "I don't care if you are full, my dear, I want my two sons in your school!" Rhoda was so stunned that she said, "Okay," and we went two over. Bea turned out to be a sweet and supportive parent—and a kick in the ass!

Each Crossroads graduate probably has his or her own favorite Cabaret moments, and mine would include: hearing for the first time Roy Orbison singing "Pretty Woman," having Zooey Deschanel sing an adapted version of "Over the Rainbow" in a tribute to Crossroads as "Over the Freeway," watching Tim Conway standing in a hole up to his waist on stage and doing calisthenics with several very tall members of Crossroads's basketball team, and watching sportscaster Al Michaels announcing the carpool madness at afternoon pickup time as if it were a sports event. Al was filmed on top of a Crossroads building looking down at the cars. The climax was announcing my wife, Mary Ann Cummins, driving down a one-way boulevard in the wrong direction—as she notoriously once did.

Another skit was a monologue delivered by Earl Pomerantz, a writer and former stand-up comic. His monologue focused on our "ugly" campus with its by-now beloved alley running through the middle. He said that Crossroads provided its privileged Westside students with something offered by no other private school: a "sense of deprivation." But amid the humor is a clear sense of pride among parents and students, with the alley symbolizing the school's sense of community, created and sustained by all.

Having celebrities as parents was often a boon to the academic program as well. As headmaster, I always taught one section of senior English. One year, when I was teaching *Death of a Salesman* to my seniors, Dustin Hoffman agreed to talk to the class about his experience playing Willy Loman. He was brilliant. When I assigned *A Streetcar Named Desire*, I called a Crossroads grandparent, Karl Malden, and invited him to my class. He had played Mitch with Marlon Brando and Jessica Tandy on Broadway and with Brando and Vivien Leigh in the film. He, too, was wonderful with the students.

On occasions, however, celebrities have presented some peculiar dilemmas. One phone call I made may illustrate such. The conversation went something like this:

Paul: "George, hi, this is Paul Cummins with a little problem I need to talk to you about."

George: "Sure, my man, what's up?"

Paul: "Well, George, it seems that your daughter may sometimes be bringing some grass to school, and I don't want to catch her, because I like her and you and want to keep her in the school."

George: "I get you, no problem."

Paul: "Well, there is an additional point, which is that your daughter may be getting the stuff from you."

George: "Well, of course, man, I don't want her buying bad shit on the streets."

Paul: "As a father, too, I understand, George, but since she may be sharing this stuff with other kids, it sort of makes you a supplier to the school."

George: "Oh, wow, I see your point. Okay, man, no more, no problem."

Paul: "Thanks, George. Please tell K not to bring stuff to school."

And so the problem was averted. George Carlin was, in fact, a wonderfully supportive parent and great talent.

Crossroads School's special atmosphere is exemplified most profoundly by the relationships between students and teachers. From the beginning, I sought to hire teachers who genuinely *liked young people*, so this quality of the school is actually no accident. We have always encouraged teachers to go beyond their subject—to teach students and not just a subject, to get to know each student, to care about his or her life. When teachers have the courage to seek relationships in their teaching, marvelous and magical things happen in and outside the classroom. Students reach, teachers go beyond the norm, and something emerges that is greater than either could have achieved alone. It can happen in a simple math assignment as well as an autobiographical essay or community service project. The key is "relationship," and the driving forces are affection and encouragement.

As I write these reflections (circa 2012–14), I now have the vantage point of how our graduates (who are returning to ten-, twenty- and even thirty-year reunions, with a fortieth [2016] rapidly approaching), view the school and its impact upon their lives. Their responses are, in a word, thrilling. Many say their years at Crossroads were transformational. They say school allowed them time and space to grow, to make mistakes, to discover interests and sometimes even passions, to be different and feel validated for these differences.

Many graduates speak fondly of this or that teacher, but most say that Mysteries or community service or the Ojai trip, or this drama production or that concert were life-changing. I tell them they were life-changing for me too. What I think I knew initially at an intuitive level—certainly at the level of risk and faith—has been, I believe, validated. As I quote Robert Frost at the beginning of this chapter: *the thing was to get now and then elated.*

CHAPTER 8

Arts and Athletics

*Through my art I am continuously trying
to explain myself to myself.*

—Herb Alpert

EARLY ON, IT SEEMED THAT Crossroads and I, as its headmaster, struggled for recognition in the education world. For example, in the admissions process I would interview prospective parents, and frequently the conversation would go something like this: "Well, we have two children. One is very bright and he/she is going to XYZ" (one of the established, prestigious private schools). "Our second child is very, well . . . very creative, and we would like him/her to attend Crossroads." Creative, of course, was often code for *not a good student* or *a behavior problem* or *we couldn't get him/her in anywhere else.* Such conversations certainly bothered me. I suppose my sense of pride was wounded by being perceived as second or third best.

Also, as mentioned earlier, other heads of schools tended to dismiss Crossroads as hippie, artsy, and generally academically inferior. This, too, rankled. Nevertheless, at a core level, I knew we were offering a first-rate and challenging curriculum, and I had to trust that in time the school would receive its just recognition. Meanwhile, I had a new idea.

Soon after Crossroads opened, we formed a mini jug band, patterned after a superb jug band I had enjoyed listening to at Oakwood School. Mary Ann Erman, soon to be my wife, was the "teacher" of the group, which had some moments of "unusual" music-making. A few years later in 1977, when quite by accident we enrolled a few good musicians, this time Mary Ann put together a lively and effective "jazz ensemble" of disparate instruments. My new idea was: why not actively seek and recruit talented musicians and create a serious classical chamber ensemble? Mary Ann and I discussed the idea, and I ran an ad in the *Los Angeles Times* announcing that scholarships were available for talented young instrumentalists. Soon after, we held auditions one Saturday morning.

Saturday arrived, and, unfortunately, Mary Ann couldn't be there, so I waited by myself for throngs of eager musicians to show up. I waited. And waited. Finally, at day's end, one little girl, Sharon Yamada, an eighth-grade applicant, appeared. She was enormously talented, sweet, polite, and intelligent. I auditioned her and told her mother we would be happy to accept her. Since the ad hadn't worked, we needed to try a different strategy. We began approaching private teachers—violin, viola, cello—offering to provide selected students with financial assistance and musical-theory instruction (which most private teachers value but do not have time to teach), as well as chamber music and music ensemble experience. Of course, we also offered a first-rate academic experience, which the public schools were finding increasingly hard to provide. Gradually, we assembled an outstanding group of musicians, many of whom (including Sharon Yamada) have gone on to distinguish themselves as solo concert artists, leading chamber music performers, and players in major symphony orchestras.

Shortly after Sharon enrolled in Crossroads, I began formulating one of my better ideas. At first, I suggested to our Board of Trustees that we create a Music Academy, a sort of school within the school. The Board thought this too radical, so I suggested, instead, that we create an arts major program in music (eventually we created majors in all the arts).

I pointed out to our board that a student interested in math could take classes from algebra to advanced calculus; a music student had no such opportunity. This idea was embraced. Thus, Mary Ann and I enlisted the advice and eventually the partnership of several USC faculty from the music department: Marianne Uszer, Nancee Cortes, and Herbert Zipper.

We created, looking back, an extraordinary curriculum, which included four years of music theory, chamber music, solo recitals, and master classes. As the enrollment grew, we realized that we were now ready to create a strong chamber ensemble.

Sharon had come to us as an eighth-grade student in the fall of 1977. She would have to wait until 1980 before we had a bona fide chamber ensemble with which she could perform. But when it finally came together, it was instantly of high quality. Initially, we arranged for two excellent students from USC's graduate conducting program to lead the ensemble: first Antonia Wilson, then Sylvain Fremeaux. A year later, Mary Ann approached Myun-whun Chung, the assistant conductor of the Los Angeles Philharmonic, in quest of a more permanent conductor. He suggested the first violist of the Los Angeles Philharmonic, Heiichiro Ohyama, who wanted to try conducting. We hired Ohyama, who proved to be an extraordinary musician and a brilliant and demanding conductor.

Under Ohyama's leadership and with continuing recruitment, we put together one of the finest high school string ensembles in the world. The quality of their playing was, and still is, astounding. Over the years we have had various artists—such as Yo-Yo Ma, André Previn, and Emanuel Ax—solo with the ensemble. Guest conductors such as Esa-Pekka Salonen, Simon Rattle, and Previn have been dazzled by their ability.

Crossroads music graduates are now distinguishing themselves all over the world. To highlight just a few, Joan Kwoun is a dazzling violin soloist; Max Levinson is a distinguished concert pianist and teacher at the Boston Conservatory; pianist Andrew von Oeyen solos with major orchestras internationally; Danielle de Niese sings with the Metropolitan Opera and with other major opera companies; Robert Chen is concertmaster of the Chicago Symphony; Sheryl Staples and Michelle Kim are associate and assistant concertmasters and soloists with the New York Philharmonic; Steven Copes is concertmaster of the Saint Paul Chamber Orchestra; and our pioneer Sharon Yamada also plays in the New York Philharmonic.

I believe that as the chamber ensemble came into its power it provided the school with a couple of new benefits. For one, it was hard to square the image of a second-rate school with the emergence of such talent and performances at the Dorothy Chandler Pavilion. In addition, as major donors all over the city would see a joint concert of the Los Angeles Philharmonic and the Crossroads Chamber Orchestra, the school's reputation as a quality institution grew. Finally, loving music as I do, hearing these young people perform Brahms and Shostakovich was simply goose-bump thrilling.

However, as proud as I became of our music program, I was aware that another love of mine needed attention—athletics.

In the fall of 1978, a coach from an inner-city school made an appointment to see me. He had heard of Crossroads. He arrived with two African American students in tow: one six feet tall and the other six foot five. Their school, he informed me, was being shut down, and he wanted his two protégés to go to Crossroads. In those days, we were not fully enrolled, and I simply accepted "financial-aid students" on a rolling-admissions basis. My theory was that an empty seat might as well be filled if a paying customer was unavailable. Financial aid, I explained to various board members on many occasions, is not an "expense." We enrolled the two seniors, Greg Washington and Doug Thomas. When they joined senior Donald McCleary and ninth-grader Kevin McCleary Jackson, we had a powerful basketball team overnight. The team went to the California Interscholastic Federation semifinals before losing a close game to Chadwick, 39–34. Being the ex-jock and lifelong basketball aficionado that I am, I found the CIF experience enormously exciting, and having come that close to winning a championship, I seduced myself into wanting to go all the way as quickly as possible.

By 1982 we had assembled a powerhouse team. Kevin was a senior and a superb point guard. He was joined by Michael Morris, a power forward; Robin Andrews, a sharp-shooting off guard; and six-foot-seven Jeff Todd, an outstanding center. The team won their league and again met Chadwick in the semifinals. We had lost to Chadwick rather decisively earlier in the year in a tournament, so I asked the coach, Elliot Turret, a rather strong personality, whether he had any plans to slow the game down. "We're going to go right at them," he said. An unrelenting full-court press and intense fast-break basketball was his approach.

The game began, and before Chadwick could call a timeout, we had surged to a 19–2 lead. I was astounded: fast-break, basket; intercepted pass, basket; stolen in-bound pass, basket; fast-break, basket . . . The crowd—and the headmaster of Crossroads—were going nuts. Chadwick, however, regrouped and by halftime had fought back to tie the game at 48–48. Our leading scorer, Robin Andrews, was so nervous that he spent halftime vomiting and had to sit out the third quarter with the "dry heaves." Kevin, Michael, and the others took over and established a quick six-point lead to begin the third quarter. From then on, the two teams traded baskets for virtually the rest of the game. Final score: 84–78. Crossroads was to be in the championship game.

The championship final was against our archrival, Montclair Prep. They were a bunch of tough white kids from the San Fernando Valley who allegedly talked racial trash to our players, causing no end of animosity. One of their players in particular, a white, All-CIF player, had provoked Michael Morris to foul him flagrantly in two previous games, resulting in free throws that beat us both times. In one of these games, he called Michael a racial name that enraged him; when this player was about to shoot a free throw, Mike walked up to him in plain sight and slapped him resoundingly across the face. It almost touched off a riot. Mike was thrown out of the game, the Montclair star sank all his shots and, of course, we looked like thugs. So, before the championship game, I went up to Mike and said, "If X calls you 'a dirty, motherf---ing n-----,' what are you going to do?"

"I'm going to smile at him," Mike replied, and went on to play a superb game.

The championship game was played in the Long Beach Sports Arena, and I was as nervous as I can ever remember being. I wanted more than anything to defeat Montclair. Why did I care so much? Perhaps because I was still struggling with my "Crossroads inferiority complex," perhaps because I had never been part of a championship team when I was a high school player. But also I knew the life struggles of some of our inner-city players, and I wanted them to have this victory—particularly because of the racial insults they had experienced. We led for most of the game but let it slip away in the final minutes. With thirty seconds left, we were down by one point, and the Montclair star (Michael's tormentor) was dribbling and stalling. Robin, our off guard, couldn't get the ball. Then Kevin went after him; Kevin pulled a sleight of hand, got the ball, and drove the length of the court for the winning basket. It was an oh-so-sweet moment.

Postscript

Our director of athletics, Chuck Ice, a notorious practical joker, saw our championship as a special opportunity to play "gotcha" with the headmaster. Forging the CIF letterhead, he delivered a letter to me calling for a hearing on an alleged eligibility issue pertaining to one of our players—a player whose status at Crossroads was a little shaky. I panicked, but then Chuck burst out laughing. "You sonofabitch," I said. The next morning he found a termination letter in his faculty mailbox. However, he didn't bite. Score one for Chuck.

While my initial motives in admitting some rather academically challenged students may have been nothing more than wanting winning teams, the students themselves had a profound impact on my thinking. As I learned more about their life situations, homes, families, neighborhoods, and subculture, I became aware of how difficult it was for them to succeed at a school like ours. I began to see that they needed substantial tutoring and a reduced course load until they became acclimated, and—most of all—they needed enormous amounts of encouragement.

As our teams started winning games, I found that other schools began criticizing Crossroads for athletic recruiting. At first I found myself defensive with vague feelings of guilt, as if we were doing something wrong in letting poor families with talented kids come to the school on financial aid. Then, mentally, I became defiant. I reasoned that if heads of other schools wanted winning teams like ours, they could jolly well ante up financial aid that matched our commitment of 10 percent.

My beliefs continued to evolve. Sports—if accompanied by an academic program of integrity—are a ticket to college for some of these students. Some of them played all four years in college, but most discovered other interests and developed career skills. Basketball, baseball, softball, and, in time, soccer, tennis, and volleyball opened the financial door to college, but college itself opened other doors to life in all its variety and possibilities. I came to believe, along with John Thompson, Georgetown University's famous coach, that it is important to reach out specifically to students from low-income families in order "to undo some of the wrongs that have been done by society." Thompson argues, "If the strong can't help the weak, who can?" (*International Herald Tribune*, August 18, 1997). So, while we grew more careful in our selection processes over the years, we continued to take risks *and* change lives.

During the 1980s another premier program emerged as well. Chuck Ice, our director of athletics, was a superior baseball coach. His knowledge of the game was second to none. When quite by accident he managed to collect a few good players in 1982, the baseball team started winning games. By 1983 we had a powerhouse team. When this group became seniors in 1985, they won the small-school CIF championship, demolishing their competition in the five playoff games, 114–22. There were nine hitters in the lineup and four excellent pitchers; one, Noah Rosen, finished the season with a 14–0 record. Also, the infield set a CIF small-school record for double plays. Chuck Ice won the championship again in 1987 and enjoyed ten years of winning teams.

In the mid-to-late 1980s, our girls' teams began attracting attention. Coach Larry Weiner's girls' basketball team won seventy-seven consecutive league games over a five-year span in the late 1980s, and I found myself loving girls' sports as much as boys' athletics. The girls' softball team, under Coach Tom Gray, won CIF championships in 1992 and 1993. Three girls from the 1992 team received athletic scholarships to play Division I college softball at Miami of Ohio, Northwestern, and Stanford. The emergence of a few superior extracurricular programs not only lifted everyone's morale but helped put our young school on the map.

The 1990s were also a time of pure joy for me in watching our youngest daughter, Emily, become an excellent athlete and a truly ferocious competitor. As the starting goalie on the soccer team, she amassed a school record: forty-three shutouts in seventy-six games and was selected on all the CIF teams in her senior year. Softball, however, was her favorite sport: she was our starting shortstop for four years and was twice a Southern California All-CIF selection. Our team, with Emily (a fresh-man) and Anna (a senior) playing together in 1991, advanced to the semifinals of our division playoffs but were shut out by an excellent pitcher. In 1992 we reached the finals, only to play the same team again and to face the same pitcher as the year before. In a large stadium before a full house, this time we won: Emily, a sopho-more, had three hits and drove in the winning run with a clutch single to left field. It was a moment to savor.

Harvard School, 1953
Varsity Football

I have thought a great deal about athletics during the last twenty-five years and confess to a profound ambivalence. I can see how playing sports benefited my daughters. I can also see how they benefited me—in fact, I see it quite regularly. A shy, withdrawn, private, "soft" little boy learned through sports about working with others, competition, overcoming fear and doing one's best, both winning and losing graciously, respecting one's opponents, and getting up without whining af-ter you have been knocked down. In retrospect, I believe my athletic experiences contributed to my effectiveness as a school leader. Yet now, as I see the growing professionalizing of pre-collegiate sports, not to mention the drug usage, macho attitudes, and pure nastiness and selfishness that so many sports engender today, I wonder whether the value they still have for our young people is not outweighed by the damage incurred. In a world increasingly desensitized to poverty and misery, in which the very membrane of the planet is under assault from profiteers who justify their attacks in the name of "competitive" economic progress, one has to wonder whether competition itself will not ultimately lead to the further degradation of people and the planet—hence, my ambivalence.

CHAPTER 9

Magic: The Key Ingredient

I don't want realism, I want Magic!

—Tennessee Williams

LONG BEFORE THE HARRY POTTER series blanketed the planet with its glorification of magical powers, I had come to believe in the positive, educational connotations of the word magic. To some it may suggest witchcraft and evil necromancy. To me it signifies enchantment and trans-rational awareness of the human spirit expressing itself in creative forms and actions. After all the tests, evaluations, and grades, what students retain are the moments of joy, the epiphanies where meaning is magically revealed. These revelations can come in simple events or in grandiose productions. They often come when a teacher is on fire, and his or her passion invades the student's very being. Such moments are not daily fare, but with great teachers they also are not rare.

With this guiding belief, I sought to hire teachers who I believed could create such moments and evoke such an atmosphere in their classrooms, theaters, or studios. Consequently, the interview process was critical. Hiring decisions often rested upon intuition—some of which turned out excitingly positive, and others, well, less so.

I recall one Saturday interview with a prospective history teacher, Jeff Cooper. At one point I asked him one of my favorite types of questions: "If you were given a six-month sabbatical on a desert island to read three historians, whom would you select?" He thought for a moment and then said, "Gibbon, Toynbee, and Herodotus." He went on to brilliantly explain why he chose these three. I was quite knocked out. I told him I would call him early next week.

At seven o'clock that evening my phone rang; it was Jeff. "Dr. Cummins," he said excitedly, "I've been thinking about it, and I think I would prefer Thucydides rather than Herodotus," and he elaborately explained why. When we hung up, I knew I had my guy! Jeff turned out to be an extraordinary teacher whose Marxist passion for ideas inspired huge numbers of students, including my daughter Anna.

I mentioned earlier that when I first observed Mary Ann teach Orff, I saw magic at work; I saw knowledge of subject matter combined with an intuitive sense of when to improvise, how to create metaphors to help students see, hear, and understand the essence of the lesson. Frequently, arts teachers have this ability, but so, too, do academic teachers if—and this is the key factor—if creating magic is what leads them to the classroom day after day. Every good teacher, like good basketball players, can tell you what it is like to be "in the zone." Finding teachers who know that zone, I believe, is the head of school's major responsibility.

Jim Hosney was such a teacher at Crossroads. I hired him in 1982 to be an English teacher. At the end of the first year he asked whether he could teach three English sections and one film class. I agreed. The following June he asked whether it could be "two and two." Soon he was teaching mostly film, and the following year he taught one Great Books class. A March 2005 article in *Vanity Fair* explained Jim's impact on a whole generation of Crossroads grads:

> One reason Hosney's former students revere him is that he never condescended to them. Back in the 80s, just as he does today, "the Hoz," as Paul Cummins calls him, also taught at the American Film Institute in Los Angeles, and because he does not drive—a point of pride with him, friends say—Crossroads students sometimes shuttled him to his class, where they discovered that Hosney was delivering the same lectures to A.F.I.'s graduate students that he was giving them.
>
> "Half of us never understood what he was talking about," Brett Morgen says. "But when you're in 9th grade and 10th grade, you're so impressionistic that even though you may not fully grasp the true meaning of a film like "Weekend" or "La Chinoise," you'd marvel at the

subversive energy and the challenge—the notion that art, and the pop medium, can serve multiple purposes."

Creating a magical environment that allows, even encourages students to discover their talents and passions often works the same way for teachers. Over the years at Crossroads this has happened often. To illustrate, Davida Wills, now Wills-Hurwin, came to Crossroads in 1983 as a dance teacher and did choreography for the drama department. Later, she became chair of the dance department and then a combined dance/drama program. Along the way, the school's drama productions became standing room only.

In 1988 the drama department put on a musical performance of *Runaways* by Elizabeth Swados. Attending the school at that time was a talented young girl, Amy Krichman, who was also blind. Davida cast Amy and choreographed the production so that everyone did their thing but also knew when and how to make certain that Amy got from point A to B to C. It was done seamlessly with Amy singing and dancing and gliding across the stage with complete confidence, grace, and joy. I discovered afterward that in rehearsals Davida had each member of the cast act out a scene or moment blindfolded so that they would be attuned to Amy's reality. That, I thought, was brilliant teaching.

Davida also found time, somehow, to write two wonderful novels about the teen years: *A Time for Dancing* and *Freaks and Revelations*. Like the graduates of the music class, Crossroads drama majors, not surprisingly, have made their mark all over the country in film and on stage. Many of these graduates say it all began in the little black-box theater just off 21st Street and the Alley.

Of course, as have most educators, I have wondered what leads one into teaching. Why did I give up making a lot of money—which I have little doubt I could have done? Why do teachers give up their evenings, weekends, and vacations correcting papers and planning lessons? I believe the overwhelming answer is to experience the elation that comes after engaging a student or students in those moments where both parties—teacher and student—have a breakthrough moment, an epiphany, a dramatic realization of something new. It is a high that is hard to describe. But the good and great teachers who know it and have tasted it once cannot help but seek it again and again. When an entire school acknowledges this is a dream to be pursued, the whole atmosphere changes. Outsiders come onto the campus and say that the electricity is palpable, that the joy and involvement of students is evident.

During my years as headmaster, I always taught one section of twelfth-grade English, and I like to believe I had some "in the zone," magical moments of my own.

One day, I recall, I was to teach a poem by Richard Wilbur entitled "Juggler." The poem begins:

> A ball will bounce, but less and less. It's not
> a light-hearted thing, resents its own resilience.
> Falling is what it loves, and the earth falls
> so in our hearts from brilliance,
> settles and is forgot.
> It takes a sky-blue juggler with five red balls
> To shake our gravity up . . .

Prior to my class I contracted for a freelance juggler to come to my class and stay around the corner out of sight until my cue. As I read the poem out loud he entered in his blue shirt, juggling four red balls (he told me he couldn't do five, but I thought the kids wouldn't mind). It was just a brief interlude, but it helped set the scene. My discussion and elucidation of the poem came alive. Such moments stay with you and, hopefully, with your students.

I also remember a class I taught during my early career. It was a twelfth-grade class of about fourteen students, very bright and responsive young boys, and we had developed a wonderful working rapport. I don't remember the precipitating event, but, somehow, I got the giggles and gradually so did they. Very soon we were all laughing. I tried to get us calmed down to return to the lesson, but I started laughing again, and so did they. This went on for a full thirty minutes, and then the bell rang. Class was over. We laughed for almost the whole class. It was memorable, delightful, and life-affirming; a metaphor for what learning and education could be and should be.

CHAPTER 10

A Constant Challenge:
The F Word

My financial problems are simple,
I'm short on money.

—Henny Youngman

I SUPPOSE THAT THE STORY of the education of a headmaster must eventually deal with the F word: *fundraising*. In the last few years, I have been told that I am an exceptional fundraiser ("A phenomenal fundraiser," according to *Buzz* magazine, November 1997). I wince internally every time I hear this said. I don't think I'm all that good. Since I've never particularly enjoyed fundraising, I have a hard time staying as focused and diligent as I should be. Whenever I am soliciting someone, it is because they have funds that I and my institution want and do not have. Consequently, there is always at least a trace of feeling as though I'm requesting a handout, as if I'm standing there with an awkwardly printed cardboard sign saying "Will work for food."

Needless to say, I like what the funds enable us to do. And when I am in the right frame of mind, I can bring a competitive spirit to the process. Sometimes I can work myself up to a contest mentality: the funds are there, someone is going to get them—why not us, if we do our preparation, strategizing, and soliciting cre-atively and engagingly.

Like many other endeavors, fundraising is a skill that comes with years of ex-perience, establishing reputation and relationships. In the early years of the school, a $500 or $1,000 gift was a cause for great celebration. We launched Crossroads School with virtually no fundraising. We rented classrooms in a Baptist church and operated a break-even budget on $45,000 in tuition dollars. We did hold one fund-raising event: a screening of documentary films donated for the evening by Pyramid Films. We charged ten and twenty-five dollar admission and screened the films at the Santa Monica Public Library; I think the evening generated about $1,000 or $1,500. Annual giving in those days was budgeted to yield about $2,000 to $3,000; in 2010–11 the total contributed income was $3,578,000. In December of 2000 we completed a $17 million capital campaign. This represented the culmination of a thirty-year process.

One of my first "big" gifts, ironically, earned me a reprimand from my chief fun-draising mentor and advisor on the Board of Trustees. I met Chuck Boxenbaum at the elementary school one Saturday morning where he, a new parent, was serving as the treasurer for a fundraising bake sale. I learned from another parent that Chuck was one of the founders of First Los Angeles Bank. I subsequently found out how lucky we were to have him at the school. He became a trustee, and I would learn more from him about fundraising than anyone else I have ever worked with. Early in our professional relationship, he gave me some pointers about solicitation. "Always," he said, "have equals ask equals": in other words, do not ask people alone, take along a major giver to ask another potential major giver. Someone who has already given is your best asker of someone else.

About this time, we had one major prospect at the school, a man who was (and is) extraordinarily wealthy and the owner of enormous real estate holdings. Chuck and I tried to coordinate our calendars for the "ask," as he was going to go with me, but finding dates convenient for everyone took a while. So one day, on the spur of the moment, I set up a meeting with the prospect all by myself. He met me in his office, where I made my brief pitch. He agreed that the school had done a fine job with his son, and he wanted to help. He went into his back office and shortly returned with a check for $10,000. I returned to my office, eager to tell Chuck the news. He said, "Idiot, Paul, he bought you off with chewing-gum money!" Had Chuck made the ask, there's no telling what the gift might have been. Thereafter, I always tried to discuss my plans with Chuck and with my development colleagues first!

Chuck Boxenbaum and others not only gave me advice and counsel, they also reached into their own pockets whenever we needed them to. Once, a building on our newly emerging city-block campus came up for sale. It was a sudden deal, and we had to act fast to put together a down payment. Chuck summoned several of his trustee colleagues to a meeting at his house, and by the end of the evening, we had the $35,000 we needed to secure the property.

I recall one fundraising meeting where a particular parent asked why parents were "expected" to give beyond an already steep tuition. Another parent, the late Ed Weinrot, gave an answer I thought profound. He said, "I give because my child today is benefiting from gifts parents gave years ago, even when they knew their child was not going to be at the school much longer. So I give today to help someone else's child benefit tomorrow; it is my way of saying 'thank you' to the parents of yesterday." If only our entire society had such an enlightened concept of posterity.

Nevertheless, in those days Crossroads was not well-positioned to play in the big fundraising ballparks; we operated with four strikes against us each time we went up to bat. Strike one: in the tenth year of the school, we still had no alumni. Students from our original eighth grade (and first senior class) had either just graduated from college or were in graduate school. Strike two: we didn't own any of our buildings; we leased five or six buildings and paid rent on each. Strike three: the parents of our students were primarily first-generation-wealth families. They were not the third- and fourth-generation-wealth families with a family tradition of philanthropy. They were just getting accustomed to acquiring and having money; giving it away was an unfamiliar concept. I soon realized that because of our school's "liberal" first-generation wealth and the absence of alumni, I would have to rely on foundations more than the more established private schools did. This was in spite of strike four: the third- and fourth-generation families who send their children to older established schools often sit on the boards of major foundations and tend to route that foundation money back to their own children's schools.

Nevertheless, the California Foundation Directory became my constant companion. I pored through its pages, searching for names I could recognize, contacts, leads, ways to get my toe in the door here or there. Once, I called a foundation where I recognized the name of a trustee as a former neighbor and friend of my sister's. I introduced myself to the foundation's secretary, who said, "Don't you recognize my voice?" "No," I said. She turned out to be a former Stanford girlfriend. We received a $5,000 grant from the foundation. But grants were not easy to come by, in part due to strike four.

Still, there were some early bits of good fortune, some exceptions to the rule. One family new to the school, Judy and Fred Warren, made a $100,000 stock transfer to our capital drive in 1980, and we had our first six-figure gift. Judy soon became a trustee and then helped organize our first Development Office.

In those days I sought desperately to secure a personal interview with this or that grant officer. I believed that I had a better chance of selling my dreams face to face, and sometimes it worked out that way. But more often, it was a matter of sending off proposals and hoping. I soon learned that the rate of positive response wasn't high, and that the "mud at the wall" theory applied: the more you throw, the more likely it is that some will stick. At first, we were fortunate to receive some helpful grants from foundations such as the William Randolph Hearst Foundation, the Mary Pickford Foundation, the Joseph Drown Foundation, the Roth Family Foundation, and the Bing Foundation. Then in 1982 we received our first major foundation support, a $100,000 grant from the Ahmanson Foundation, and (also in 1982) a $100,000 grant from the W.M. Keck Foundation.

In retrospect, the past decades of fundraising have brought benefits to me and to the school far beyond the funds raised. The school has gained friends and supporters whose investments in our dreams have brought joy and a sense of unusual accomplishment for them personally. For many people, having money is not an unadulterated pleasure; in fact, I have noticed that some people with substantial wealth have a concomitant need to find meaning in their lives beyond their money. A young school like Crossroads often applied the donated funds to visible, tangible projects for which the donors felt a direct responsibility and immediate sense of accomplishment. Lately I have learned to see my fundraising less as begging and more as providing donors with a unique opportunity to make a difference. This outlook, of course, dramatically changed the mindset that I brought to the "ask."

For me, the beyond-dollar benefits were many. For one, I learned a great deal about how my city, Los Angeles, worked and didn't work. You can't submit a grant proposal of your own without researching what this or that foundation has given to in the past, and often the research leads to side roads or collaborations to explore.

Over the years, as I acquired a reputation for having become a good fundraiser, other, and often younger, heads of nonprofits were coming to me for advice and assistance. When I found their projects exemplary, I would call a friend heading this or that foundation and ask them to meet with one of these nonprofit organizations. I remember, for example, often calling Lee Walcott, the head of the Ahmanson Foundation, and after a while when I would call, Lee would say with a tone of mock exasperation, "So, Paul, now who do you want me to give money to?" However, I could tell that Lee and his foundation associates respected my efforts to help others and not always just try to hit them up for my own projects.

Finally, because major donors were so instrumental to the success of our ventures, I spent a great deal of time getting to know key individuals. Frequently, this led to genuinely collaborative friendships. If the project was exciting, then the project itself became the prize. When things were in balance, the donors' donation and my administration of the donations blended together, and the net success was two-fold: the children and the school grew, and we—grantor and grantee—experienced the satisfaction of watching the project unfold. The creation of Crossroads School, with its rich and diverse programs, and later New Roads School and the P.S. Arts program of the Crossroads Community Foundation were such experiences. They brought joy and satisfaction to me and to hundreds of donors. Truly the blessings of giving were in receiving.

CHAPTER 11

The Flowering of Crossroads: From Experimental to Progressive

Twenty years from now you will be more disappointed by the things you didn't do than by the ones you did do. So throw off the bowlines. Sail away from the safe harbor. Catch the trade winds in your sails. Explore. Dream. Discover.

—Mark Twain

IN JULY OF 1984 I sat at a luncheon in Washington, D.C., listening to a speech by President Reagan, having just received an award on behalf of Crossroads School, which the U.S. Department of Education had selected as one of "sixty exemplary schools in America." At a reception for the award winners the previous evening, I was making small talk with the headmaster of the prestigious Andover Academy, when he mentioned that his school prided itself on being able to offer "more than three-quarters of an acre per student." I tried to hold off a choking fit and decided not to inform him that at our Crossroads campus, we would be hard-pressed to offer three-quarters of an acre for the entire student body of 600!

Gradually in the 1980s I formulated my "five other solids" theory, which I believe has made a contribution to the educational community dialogue. Yes, I would acknowledge, history, English, science, mathematics, and foreign languages are essential ingredients in any curricula. But equally important, I would affirm, are the five other solids: human development, physical education, community service/ action, the arts, and environmental education. In fact, these five others have the supreme virtues of being experiential and hands-on. In short, they engage students in ways that the "big five" often do not. The "five others" are at the heart of Crossroads's success and, I believe, its soul.

I don't know whether the exemplary-school award was the turning point, but sometime around the mid-1980s, Crossroads turned a corner: no longer a "hippie, progressive, artsy, flaky, unstructured, liberal" school, Crossroads was slowly reaping the benefits of an image shift. I was, and still am, ambivalent about this process. One the one hand, I had felt a little like a kid from the other side of the tracks when the "elite" social circles of Los Angeles were openly snubbing or being condescending to Crossroads; yet, on the other hand, I wanted people to value Crossroads for what it was and is—a progressive, innovative school with a more inclusive and diverse student population and holistic program than most so-called "traditional" prep schools. The reality was, and is, that Crossroads is highly structured and highly academic, even though it does not necessarily appear to be. Kids wear funky clothes, call their teachers by their first names, challenge their teachers in class, and between classes they hang out in an alley that divides the two rows of buildings on campus. It doesn't look the way an "exemplary" school is supposed to look.

Gradually, however, perceptions changed. The word of mouth was that not only do Crossroads kids learn a lot and get into good colleges, but they *enjoy school*. Some parents removed their children from "traditional" schools that were not working for their child, reluctantly swallowed their pride, and enrolled the kids in Crossroads. Time and time again a depressed, underachieving student would come alive, to the delight of his or her parents. One senior class after another would go to leading colleges, and most seniors were receiving acceptances from 70 and 80 percent of the schools to which they applied. Virtually 100 percent went on to college, and many would write back to report that they had arrived well prepared. (One student who went to one of the UC campuses complained during her first few weeks there, "I don't think it's too much to ask that my college be at least as demanding as my high school.")

Applications to the school increased each year. People who had once looked upon Crossroads with mild disdain were now attempting to use "influence," offering to "help" the school in any way they might, to enhance their child's chances of acceptance. One call, from a well-known Hollywood figure and former Crossroads parent, came in August with the request that I find room for four children of a business associate. "X," I said, "we're full."

He replied, "You can make it happen!" When I explained that we truly were full, he told me his associate was prepared to contribute $250,000 to the school.

I said, "That is very nice, but we are truly full."

He then paused and said, "Per child!" I must confess I had a rather strong twinge, flutter, whatever, but stayed the course. Sometime between the Reagan luncheon and the late 1980s, Crossroads became an "established" school. Our new challenge was how to maintain its institutional soul amid the sweet smell of success.

During this time, the press also began paying attention to Crossroads. A variety of newspaper articles also helped "establish" the school. In 1985 the *Los Angeles Times* ran an extensive lead article that quoted an educational consultant as follows: "The quality of their programs in the arts in my experience has no peers." The consultant, a twenty-three-year headmaster, Len Richardson, went on to say that the orchestra's level of performance was as much an achievement of the school's atmosphere of mutual respect as it was of recruitment of talent. He continued, "Sometimes informality leads to sloppiness, but at Crossroads, it seems to balance the tension that any kind of excellence creates."

These articles as well as television coverage helped to confirm Crossroads's coming of age, and as Crossroads continued to evolve, so did my own personal and family life.

Julie, Paul, Anna
Maryann, Liesl, and Emily

I had first driven up Palm Drive in Palo Alto in September of 1955 as a freshman at Stanford. Now, thirty-six years later, in September of 1991, I was driving up it again, this time with Mary Ann and our daughter Anna, who was eagerly anticipating beginning her college years. As we drove past my old dormitory, Wilbur Hall, I was flooded with nostalgia. Then, after unloading all the luggage and boxes, Mary Ann and I returned to the car. Anna kissed us goodbye and skipped back to the dorm, excited about meeting her new classmates. We drove to the freeway in silence, and I found that my tears flowed gently but persistently for the next half hour or so. Letting go . . . after eighteen years of her daily presence and of tucking her into bed and kissing her goodnight every night of the year, I would now be returning to a home with one empty bedroom and with Emily, my tenth-grade daughter soon to follow. Letting go . . . I had heard other parents describe the experience for years, but their words never fully penetrated my consciousness. Now I was enmeshed in the process. It is, of course, a process that is natural and inevitable, though coming to terms with it was a major challenge for me.

About this time, I had begun thinking of another possibility—perhaps even need—for letting go. In 1991 Crossroads School held a twenty-year celebration during which I was honored by the school community. I recalled that a friend had once said to me, "No head should stay at one school for more than ten years." Here I was going past twenty years at Crossroads. Was I getting stale? Wouldn't a new and different vision be healthy for the school? Besides, I was getting tired of the endless cycle of meetings, conferences, committees, interviews, and evening obligations and was also discovering that my new gravitational pull to connect with local public schools was becoming more and more time-consuming. I met with Roger Weaver, my associate headmaster, and suggested that we consider a new possibility.

with Roger Weaver, my successor at Crossroads, and our pal
Michele Hickey

Roger and I had met in 1982 when he accepted the job of assistant headmaster. We met, he often reminds me, at the Long Beach Sports Arena, where Crossroads was playing in its first CIF basketball finals. I was slightly crazed with nervousness and excitement, and it is a wonder that I seemed coherent enough to convince him I was a serious educator, not simply a sports lunatic. In any event, he chose to become assistant headmaster at Crossroads over more traditional private schools, and we began our longtime partnership and friendship. After a number of years, I felt so confident in his judgment that I asked him to become associate headmaster and to take on even more responsibility. We spoke as if we had one voice. Therefore, when I thought it was time to redefine my relationship to the school, Roger was the natural choice to become headmaster, and a smooth transition seemed possible if we could work it out together.

According to conventional wisdom, having the founding headmaster hang around when a new headmaster begins is a prescription for disaster. Roger and I had seen and heard of such horror stories, and we determined that if this shift that involved him becoming head of school (a new title for him) and me becoming president of the school were to occur, we would need to plan with extraordinary care and diligence. We enlisted the support of Barbara Hanna, the school's mental health coordinator, and in 1992 we began an eighteen-month planning process that would lead to the transfer of power, which would officially begin on July 1, 1994.

We met with the coordinator regularly and began listing current and new responsibilities. Even more importantly, we began making a list of conflicts, hurt feelings, issues, and problems of every kind that we could imagine might occur. Making admissions choices, we knew, could be a sore spot so, basically, we agreed that I would need to stay pretty much hands-off. It was not easy. Right off the bat, Roger felt he would have to occupy my office, which was in everyone's mind "the headmaster's office." It was like asking me to move out of my house: this had been my office for over twenty years! However, his logic prevailed, and we decided that I would move to an office in another wing of the administrative building.

It was also difficult selling the idea to Mary Ann, who felt that my role as headmaster was so much a part of the school that somehow my stepping away would cause a fundamental disturbance in the system. I was resolute but had moments of weakness. I was particularly shaken when a good friend, Mike Babcock, the headmaster of Pasadena Poly, an excellent prep school, resigned, intending to go to work for the public sector. Mike had no sooner made his announcement and his school had no sooner begun a search for his replacement, than he changed his mind. I spoke to him, and he said he realized he had made a terrible mistake: he didn't really want to give up being headmaster of a school he had been with for such a long time. His Board of Trustees reinstated him, and Mike said that a personal disaster had been averted. Was I making an equally terrible mistake? Would I too regret my decision? I had a few sleepless nights but finally decided that my own ambitions and talents would be better served by moving beyond the boundaries of the school, and that Crossroads's long-term health would benefit from an orderly transition with the kind of continuity Roger and I could supply. So I put my anxieties aside, and we continued our preparations. Soon we made our various announcements to the student and parent body and to the larger community.

On June 30, 1994, nearly three years after driving Anna to Stanford for the first time, I left my old office, having packed boxes and boxes of books and files and artifacts of all kinds, and began my summer vacation. Roger moved into the headmaster's office, and in August, while my new office was being remodeled for my return as president of Crossroads, I set off for China.

China was a wonderful diversion from the sadness and anxiety I felt at giving up my headmastership. Anna (who had just completed her junior year at Stanford) and I flew to Beijing. We joined Herbert Zipper, the famed musician and Holocaust survivor (who was also my surrogate father and whose biography I had written). My purposes in traveling to China were threefold: to participate in a book signing of a Chinese edition of my biography of Herbert (*Dachau Song*); to audition music students who wanted to come to Crossroads; and, of course, to be with Anna and see China.

**with Herbert Zipper
in Vienna**

Because Herbert had conducted and taught Chinese orchestras for more than ten years, my biography of him was well-received, and I was treated as a sort of dignitary. Superb food, a personal driver, and elaborate arrangements for us to see the wonders of Beijing were all daily fare. The parents of one of Mary Ann's piano students, Yi Dong, were gracious hosts, taking Anna and me to the Great Wall, the Summer Palace, and a "lost" but recently discovered underground palace. Mary Ann had a commitment in Los Angeles, but she and Emily planned to meet Anna, Herbert, and me in Europe after we left China.

Anna and I had heard many stories about the Beijing Conservatory of Music from Herbert, but the reality was more impressive than we ever could have anticipated. The building itself was dull, almost like an army barracks or a slum tenement. However, inside we found one dorm room after another full of laughing and smiling children practicing instruments ranging from violins to ancient and exotic mandolin-like treasures. In one room, a little boy was propped up on about five books to reach the piano keys, but how he could play! It was astounding. It also made me wonder whether I was relinquishing my headmastership too soon, before we had fully developed our own music program and arranged for its sustainability. I realized, however, that second-guessing my decision was an ongoing temptation that I must resist.

During this trip, I recruited three wonderful students for Crossroads's music program: Nu Lin, a cellist from Tianjin, and from the Beijing Conservatory, Zhen Ni, a violinist, as well as Mu Rui, a pianist. All three made wonderful contributions to the music program.

From Beijing, we flew to Vienna for a book signing of a German edition of *Dachau Song* and for further sightseeing. In Vienna, Mary Ann and Emily, our other daughter, joined Anna, Herbert, and me. We visited Herbert's childhood home, and he pointed out where his next-door neighbor, Egon Schiele, had lived; we visited Doblinger's, a famous music store that displayed the German edition of my book in the front window; we attended a concert of one of Herbert's recent compositions; and we visited his favorite countryside lake, Gosau, a European treasure. We also left Herbert for a week and traveled as a family to Prague and Budapest.

In retrospect, the immense distances we covered during this time probably helped me forget about Crossroads and my lingering sense of loss. I returned in August eager to begin my new responsibilities as president and to fix up my new office. However, Mary Ann and I also had to prepare for another "letting go." In late August, Emily packed her luggage and set off for her freshman year at Northwestern. A new role, an unfamiliar office on a new campus, and now an empty nest at home.

From President to Retirement from Crossroads

It's a poor sort of memory
that only works backwards.

—Lewis Carroll

THE YEARS FROM 1994 TO 2004 were indeed years of change and new ventures, but they also gave me an opportunity to observe Crossroads's growth and achievements. As president of Crossroads, my evenings were more my own, and given the release from the day-to-day headmaster's duties, I had enough distance to separate the forest from the trees. It was, I came to see, a rather verdant forest.

Staying on at the school for another ten years allowed me to see what the students truly valued, and as ten- and then twenty- and even thirty-year reunions took place, more and more graduates returned to give testimony to what they valued, even loved about the school. Yes, they valued their academics and felt well-prepared for college. After many superb teachers at Crossroads, many graduates said they found college a bit of a letdown in that the teachers were often less encouraging, less personal, and less engaging.

They also found the academic specialties at Crossroads unique. The classics program, for example, was blessed with a parade of extraordinary teachers who were delighted to find a middle and high school that championed Latin and Greek: Latin is required at grades seven and eight and offered at nine through twelve, and Greek is offered at grades nine through twelve. The film program, headed by a brilliant teacher, Jim Hosney, inspired two decades of students, and his courses in American film, French film, etc., became legend at the school.

Former music majors wax ecstatic over the training they received. The four-year theory program, taught by Mary Ann Cummins and Warren Spaeth, enabled them, they all agree, to sail through theory at Juilliard, New England Conservatory, Curtis, and the like. Also, as mentioned earlier, Crossroads music grads are now in most major symphony orchestras in the country. In addition, visual arts and drama majors are making their marks in the art and drama worlds. Drama majors will say that teachers such as Davida Wills-Hurwin, Scott Weintraub, Peggy O'Brien, and Ginny Russell changed their lives; while visual arts majors will point to teachers such as Pam Posey, Lucia Vinograd, Zelda Zinn, and Vernon Salyers as having inspired their own careers and values.

Beyond the academics were what I dubbed the "five other solids." The so-called core solids—English, history, math, science, foreign languages—are clearly central to a college prep curriculum. But no less important, I believe, are the five other solids: community service/action, human development, physical education, the arts, and outdoor/environmental education. One or more of these are often areas that fully engage students and provide the joy and sustenance for their day-to-day schooling. We do students a disservice in schools across the country when we deny them any or all of these five other solids. At Crossroads each of these five others was developed in a full department with a wide variety of offerings. It was clear that when a student discovered herself in one area, life and vitality began to infuse all other activities. Consequently, providing the richest, most diverse curriculum possible maximizes the opportunities for each student to find his or her passion.

During the years from 1994 to 2004, I used Crossroads as my home base to launch P.S. Arts, create the New Visions Foundation, and co-create New Roads School as well as various other projects to be discussed in succeeding chapters. However, around 2000–01, I decided it was time to move on from Crossroads. There was no external pressure. I was getting along fine with the board and with Roger, and my community work was, I believe, a source of pride for the school. Nevertheless, it felt like it was time to relocate and start some new ventures separate from Crossroads. Initially, my family was sad and even tried to talk me out of it, but they, too, soon came to see what I saw.

Michele Hickey, Roger Weaver, and others began to prepare for my last year and for a proper send-off. A parent, Mary Farrell, collected a special history of the school through interviews with many people, including my daughters and wife. A luncheon for many friends and colleagues was organized to honor me by focusing on issues of social justice, with Jared Diamond as the guest speaker. Also, the school's annual fundraising event (which in 2002 was a Cabaret) focused upon my career, with Henry Winkler, "The Fonz," impersonating a hippie Paul Cummins-like headmaster. It was great fun. The finale was a tribute event on June 15, 2002, at the Santa Monica Miramar Hotel.

Soon after the Miramar event, I began hauling my books and files over to my new office on the New Roads campus and prepared for my new life. For several weeks, and even on occasion now, I find myself unconsciously pulling into the Crossroads campus where I worked for thirty-two years. But new projects presented themselves, and almost immediately my new education was well under way.

Before picking up on my post-Crossroads years, 2004 to today, I offer the story of how I became an educator, and from where the dreams of starting a new school evolved. In short, I offer a flashback to the years from 1937, when I was born, to May of 1970, when this book began.

The Road to Becoming a Headmaster

1937–1970

Long ago and far away
I dreamed a dream one day,
And now . . .

—Ira Gershwin

CHAPTER 12

The Early Years, 1937–1955:
Go West, Midwesterners

I could tell you my adventures—
beginning from this morning . . .
but it's no use going back to yesterday,
because I was a different person then.

—Lewis Carroll

"**They've changed it,**" **the sloppy** drunk Gay Langland (Clark Gable) says to Roslyn (Marilyn Monroe) in *The Misfits*, bemoaning the loss of a simpler, more honest, down-to-earth time when men could work outdoors, oblivious to the white-collar, gray-flannel-suit world of conformity and greed. Gabe's comment could also serve as an epitaph for the 1950s, the decade of my adolescence. It was indeed a simpler time. I graduated from high school never having heard the words "marijuana" or "ecology," and, though we swaggered and bragged to suggest otherwise, most of my classmates and our girlfriends were virgins. We drank beer (and only beer) at parties, we stayed out late driving around Los Angeles unafraid to go just about anywhere in town after midnight, "made out" in drive-in movies with angora dice knitted by our girlfriends hanging from our rearview mirrors, and watched Doris Day, Jimmy Stewart, and June Allyson movies. My public junior high school had full-time teachers in music, art, theater, physical education (four of them), wood shop, electrical shop, drafting, and crafts. Today, virtually none of these special-ties exists. I went from an almost all-white sixth grade to a fully racially mixed seventh grade with only the fear that my Levi's tag would be ripped off my back pocket. There were no gangs as such at this junior high. Though there were racially segregated "clubs," for the most part we competed only in sports. Fights at lunch or after school were infrequent and conducted with fists, rarely with knives, and almost never with guns. Yes, "they've changed it." I grew up in a very different time.

I was born in Evanston, Illinois, on September 9, 1937, but I moved with my fa-ther, mother, and sister to Fort Wayne, Indiana, by the time I was two. We lived in a pleasant, middle-class small town. I remember our Victory Garden during World War II and accompanying my mother to the meat locker for our weekly rations. I remember playing kick-the-can on neighborhood streets lighted by streetlamps whose glow was augmented by fireflies in the dusk. In winter I broke icicles off ga-rage roofs, licking their cool smoothness while walking to school bundled in several layers of clothing. I fed squirrels at our kitchen window and made model Flying Ti-ger airplanes of balsa wood, paper, and glue. I remember Hoagy Carmichael's "Old Buttermilk Sky" and seeing films such as *Wake Island* (my unwitting introduction to jingoism and racism, inflamed by hatred of World War II enemies) and *Cover Girl*, starring Rita Hayworth (which engendered my first sexual stirrings that I can recall—and has haunted me ever since with the song "Long Ago and Far Away").

During these early years in Indiana, I was blessed with parents who gave me the most crucial early-childhood gift: unconditional love. Though my parents expected me to do my best in whatever I did, I also knew I was valued simply for being me. My mother also made all our dinners family occasions. My father played ball with my friends and me, read to me, and sang my sister and me to sleep with gentle lullabies.

I remember clearly our summer vacations in upper Michigan. We took a ferry to Mackinac Island, then drove through white birch-tree-lined roads to a resort that featured log cabins surrounding a small lake and a family lodge with an out-door swimming pool. The other children and I would make forts in the woods, try to catch frogs, and visit the Paul Bunyan Memorial Park. At night, we would sometimes shine flashlights on the bears down in the garbage dump, and my sister and I would hold onto my father for dear life.

Everywhere in Indiana the influence of basketball was apparent. There were bas-kets mounted on garage doors, packed Friday-night high school games, and pickup games at recess. My father even set up a small basket for me in our low-ceilinged basement. I was shooting hoops at age two. Fort Wayne had a minor-league basket-ball team, the Zollner Pistons, and my dad took me to see them play. I remember a feisty guard, Bobby McDermott, famous for his two-handed half-court shots, and his fiery temper, which led to his frequently being ejected from games. My dad was also a Joe Louis fan, and we would listen to Don Dunphy's blow-by-blow radio accounts, which made every jab sound like a shattering punch. I also remember my sister Mimi and her friends, wearing their bobby sox, shrieking whenever Frank Sinatra came on the radio.

Me—
Age 7–8

I played touch football with my dad and my neighborhood pals, Tom and Jerry, and their dad: they were Notre Dame, and we were Northwestern. We each won about half the time, which was considerably better than Northwestern was doing in those days. I took my leather football to bed with me, and Otto Graham was my hero.

I clearly remember April 12, 1945, the day President Franklin Delano Roosevelt died. My parents tried to be good citizens and express proper sadness, but they also felt a Republican sense of relief that this SOB was finally gone. In our house, the death of FDR, the atomic bomb, the end of World War II, and Harry Truman's presidency were subordinated to a new topic: our impending move to California. The admonition "Go West, young man" had captured my father's imagination.

We journeyed to California in 1947 via the railroads on the Super Chief. My father started his own company and began buying real estate in West Los Angeles. Soon he was developing his land with gas stations and restaurants as well as office and apartment buildings. Within one year of our arrival in California, my father moved us again, this time from our small home in Beverly Hills to 310 North Carmelina Avenue in a wealthy West Los Angeles neighborhood known as Brentwood. For $35,000 he purchased a 1.5-acre, five-bedroom house with a long driveway lined by orange trees and graced with camellias and roses. (This home sold for $5,800,000 in 2012.) In time, he hired a Japanese gardener, an African-American domestic servant (whom my parents referred to as our "colored maid"), and several Mexican workers to carry out various garden projects. I remember being secretly embarrassed by our fancy house and feeling particularly uncomfortable about the presence of various minorities working around the house. Somehow, deep inside me, it didn't seem fair that we had so much, and they were required to serve us.

I went to Horace Mann, a Beverly Hills public school, for fourth grade, then to Brentwood Public School for fifth and sixth grades, then to Emerson, a public junior high, for grades seven and eight. By then my father had a gold Cadillac El Dorado and my mother a white Cadillac Coupe de Ville. I made them drop me off two blocks from school, intuiting that in a public junior high school I would be a lot safer not being branded as a "rich boy." Some of my friends were from low-income Mexican families, and I tried to keep my family's wealth a secret from them.

As a child I was an avid reader. I particularly loved books about animals, like the Doctor Dolittle series; Thornton Burgess books, such as *Blacky the Crow* and *Bowser the Hound*; and the Albert Payson Terhune series, such as *Lad: A Dog and Lad of Sunnybank*. Then one summer day in 1948, my mother and I stopped at a drugstore in Brentwood, and the cover of a paperback on a book rack caught my eye. It was *Lucky to be a Yankee*, the autobiography of Joe DiMaggio. My mom bought it for me, and Joe became my newest hero, along with Otto Graham and Bobby McDermott. Though I was only eleven, I became determined to become a sports star. Now reading took a back seat to sports. When I entered junior high school, I also entered a six-year intellectual wasteland. Emerson Junior High was a boring, overcrowded school with few inspired teachers at best. One English teacher browbeat us into reading *Julius Caesar* and memorizing Mark Antony's funeral oration, but that was just about it for intellectual stimulation. I daydreamed, doodled, stared at two girls in particular, and marked time until recess, lunch, and after school.

By the end of eighth grade, both of my parents had noticed that I was bringing home very little school work and receiving low grades in deportment, so they enrolled me in Harvard, a private boys' military school, in 1951. I did little more homework there over the next four years, but at least classes were small. I learned to be polite to my teachers and how to feign a "sincere" interest in my classes, a skill that enabled me to compile a B-minus grade point average. My real interests were sports and girls.

By my senior year I was excelling in both football and basketball at a small-high-school level. In football, I threw ten or twelve touchdown passes, was voted co-MVP, and led our team to a 7–2 record. In basketball, I was the captain and high scorer, and my big moment came in the first round of the playoffs when I hit a twenty-foot shot at the buzzer to win the game. My father was convinced that I would go on to be a college star. Trusting his judgment, I had no idea of the painful shock that the jump to the college level would entail.

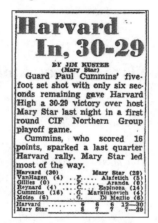

Harvard In, 30-29

BY JIM KUSTER
(Mary Star)

Guard Paul Cummins' five-foot set shot with only six seconds remaining gave Harvard High a 30-29 victory over host Mary Star last night in a first round CIF Northern Group playoff game.

Cummins, who scored 16 points, sparked a last quarter Harvard rally. Mary Star led most of the way.

Harvard (30)		Mary Star (29)
VanHagen (4)	F.	Alafetich (5)
Gillies (0)	F.	Aranda (0)
Reynard (4)	C.	Espinoza (14)
Cummins (16)	G.	Markinkovich (4)
Molso (6)	G.	Di Merlio (6)

Harvard	6	6	6	12—30
Mary Star	8	7	7	7—29

During the 1950s my father's business world was mushrooming. He was acquiring properties and businesses at a remarkable rate. He was also spending an enormous amount of time away from home, working long hours and weekends, drinking too much, and neglecting his marriage. Though I loved him dearly, I began to see how difficult their marriage was becoming for my mother. Nevertheless, when I left home to go to college, I had many of my father's values firmly instilled in me, along with his "plans" for my life. If asked what I was planning to do in college, I would answer "play football, study pre-law, go to law school, then go to work with my dad to help him manage his business." It was a quaint and comforting set of ideas, but it didn't quite work out that way. In any event, in early September of 1955 I left my Brentwood home in buoyant spirits and drove my Chevy Bel Air to Palo Alto.

CHAPTER 13

Stanford University, 1955–1957:
The Great Awakening

. . . For golden friends I had,
For many a rose-lipt maiden
And many a lightfoot lad.

—A.E. Housman,
"With Rue My Heart Is Laden"

STANFORD UNIVERSITY, SEPTEMBER OF 1955. The palm-lined road leading up
to the main quadrangle of classrooms was an awe-inspiring sight, especially to a
seventeen-year-old naïf. After checking into my dormitory and attending a few orientation meetings, I went to sign up for courses. While I stood in line, a guy next
to me introduced himself. "Hi, Jon Harris," he said, and we shook hands. He was
a skinny redhead with a long neck that made him look a bit like the stereotypical
geek. "What are you reading these days?" he asked me.

I looked at him with a blank expression and said, "What do you mean? Classes
haven't started yet, have they?" He shook his head in disbelief—that someone admitted to Stanford could be so dumb. I got into Stanford probably because I had
participated in lots of high school activities—senior class president, prefect, football MVP, basketball captain and MVP, etc. I was really ignorant. I didn't read. I
think I read two novels in all my high school years, and I generally relied on Classic

Comics when writing book reports on Dickens or Hemingway. I was interested in sports and girls—in that order.

Jon Harris and I began to banter and, to my surprise, I found myself liking him. He was not the cool, jock-type of guy I was used to hanging around with, yet somehow we connected. God knows why he took an interest in me. Perhaps he recognized in me raw material ready for shaping. After I signed up for classes, he said, "Come on over to the bookstore; I want to get you a book." We walked to the bookstore, and he bought me a paperback copy of George Orwell's *Animal Farm*. That moment changed my life forever. After I read the book, Jon began explaining its allegory: the history of Russia, Karl Marx, and Communism versus capitalism. He told me that *Animal Farm* is an anti-Utopian novel and that the various pigs represented Stalin, Trotsky, and a blend of Marx and Lenin. I was not only intrigued by the depth of this little "beast fable," I was hooked. Jon then bought me Salinger's *The Catcher in the Rye*, which I read almost in a single sitting, mesmerized by Holden Caulfield's sense of alienation and his honesty. Like all teenagers, I too had a vague sense of the phoniness and hypocrisy of society, but here was an accurate description of my feelings in adolescent vernacular. Next, Jon selected another Orwell masterpiece, this time the dystopian novel *1984*. In the five to seven days before classes had begun, I had read three books—one more than I had read in four years of high school. All this was heady stuff.

Freshman football was another matter. After graduating from high school, I had spent the summer of 1955 in Redlands, California, working for the Los Angeles Rams. My dad had pulled some strings to get me the job. I was the team's water boy, practice flunky, and all-purpose go-fer. My dad had thought that this would give me a chance to work out, get some tips, and prepare for freshman football. The job was interesting enough: catching extra points for Les Richter, playing catch with Norm Van Brocklin, chatting with Tank Younger and "Deacon" Dan Towler, and receiving pointers from Billy Wade on ball handling. But Redlands was hot and lonely. I lifted weights, ate at the "thin man's training table" in order to put on weight (I went from 140 to a "massive" 155 pounds), gained accuracy by throwing footballs through auto tires swinging from goalposts, and, despite the stifling heat, ran wind sprints twice a day.

I arrived at the Stanford locker room for freshman football feeling optimistic but apprehensive too. There was no coach to greet me, and I thought it odd that a quarterback wouldn't have received a notebook of plays to learn. But I was shy and waited to be told what to do. There was, at least, a locker with my name on it. So I suited up, tried to meet a few guys—most of whom were surly and unfriendly (I later surmised that only "big-name" recruits received friendly welcomes)—and went out to the field. We began with 100-yard wind sprints. Possessing average speed, I finished the first five or six in the middle of the pack. Then I began moving up in sprints seven through ten, and I noticed guys dropping out and vomiting on the field. We went from over a hundred players to about seventy in three days.

Summer 1955—
working for the Los Angeles Rams

About the fifth or sixth day, I was put into a scrimmage for the first time. I still hadn't received a playbook and had to whisper to a halfback to ask him what I should do. My first pass play was even more embarrassing. I went back to pass, but because the linemen were much bigger than I was used to in high school, I couldn't locate my receiver. Then bam! I was slammed to the ground. The coach shouted at me to get rid of the ball sooner, which I tried to do with little success in the next play. My pass floated out near the receiver but was intercepted. The coach yelled, "This isn't high school, sonny; you've got to zip it in three seconds up here." On the ninth day of practice, I was moved to safety on the fifth- or sixth-string defense. On one play, during a scrimmage, the line opened a huge hole, and all of a sudden the fullback, a huge guy, came charging up the middle right at me, with a ten-yard head of steam. I waited and slammed into him and did everything I had been taught— hit him low and hard. He flattened me and went on to score.

The next day, I was returned to quarterback and put into a scrimmage. I went back to pass. One of my offensive linemen missed his block, and a rusher hit me just as I passed, driving me into the ground, shoulder first. I lay there in pain with a separated shoulder. A cab took me to the Palo Alto clinic. That was it. My locker, I learned later, was cleaned out, my name scratched off various lists, and my football career at Stanford ended as it had begun—with no one paying a bit of attention to me.

After my exam at the clinic, the doctor gave me painkiller, told me a pin wouldn't be necessary, and put my arm in a sling. I took a bus back to my dorm. My shoulder ached, and I was apprehensive about calling my dad. I knew how much he wanted me to succeed. He had been a second-string quarterback in college, and I knew his fantasy was to have me become the college star he had hoped to be. I loved my dad beyond measure and would have done anything I could to make him proud, but there was a simple problem here: I just wasn't able to play college ball at this level. Finally, I summoned up my courage and called him. We exchanged the predictable remarks: "Tough luck, son, maybe next year."

"Sure, dad, well, we'll see." I burst into tears as I hung up, but I soon realized that these were tears of relief—that I didn't have to do this anymore. Football did, however, teach me some valuable lessons for use later on. I did learn how to get knocked down and get back up. I learned how to experience physical pain but overcome it and go on. I learned how to compete and how to try to be smarter than one's opponent—not how to harm him, but just how to outsmart him. I also deeply believe that my lifelong search for fairness—from the elementary school playground all the way up to the workings of society as a whole—derives directly from the rules I was taught to live by on the playing field.

Meanwhile, back on campus, while my friend Jon tried to be sympathetic to my injury, he confessed that he was pleased that I could now stop wasting time with this silly, barbaric game. Instead, under his tutelage I could spend more time remedying my incredible illiteracy. He not only continued to feed me books (Voltaire, Dostoevsky, Unamuno), but he began introducing me to music as well, especially his favorite genre and period: New Orleans jazz. Johnny Dodds, George Lewis, Louis Armstrong, Kid Ory, Jelly Roll Morton—these and others were his heroes, and I came to enjoy them too. I tried to display some musical knowledge of my own by playing Artie Shaw and Benny Goodman records for Jon, but he dismissed them as "noodlers," not in the same league as Dodds and Lewis.

In a very real sense, while Jon was my first teacher at Stanford, I soon came under the enormous influence of a truly spectacular college professor, Daniel Smith, who taught Western Civilization. Smith was an untenured instructor that I have since tried unsuccessfully to locate. His class was extraordinary. He lectured, ranted, and asked barbed questions; he paced back and forth on his platform, peering out at us from behind thick glasses, occasionally falling off the edge of the platform with his arms flailing (none of us dared to crack a smile). During the first week of class he asked a question, and I blithely raised my hand. He nodded at me and I gave my answer. With a sneer, he spat, "My God, what a pedestrian comment." After class, I went to the library to look up *pedestrian*. From his tone I recognized that I had been insulted, but I didn't know how. In the dictionary, under *pedestrian* I found "someone who walks in the streets." I was still baffled. I mentioned the incident to Jon, who shook his head as if to say, "Paul, you're hopeless—you're too dumb even to understand people's insults."

A few days later, I raised my hand again, this time tentatively, and tried again to answer a question. The same result. This time he dismissed me with "What a juvenile observation." This pattern continued throughout the fall, into the winter quarter, and even into spring quarter. I was determined to earn Professor Smith's respect. I would read an entire book between a Monday and Wednesday class just so that my answer to one question would meet with his approval. The insults continued: "asinine," "superficial," "banal," and so on. But I noticed in late winter quarter that the insults had moderated, and in early spring it happened: I answered a question and he nodded in affirmation. This was better than scoring six touchdowns.

On the final day of class, I wanted to thank him but couldn't think of how to go about it. Hesitantly, I started to leave the room. "Cummins," he called out.

"Yes, sir?" I said, quickly approaching his platform.

"What are you going to major in?" he asked. I said I didn't know. "You might consider history," he pronounced.

I smiled and said, "Thank you." I left the classroom and literally ran to the registrar's office to declare a history major. Wherever you are, Daniel Smith, here is a heartfelt thank you.

During my freshman year, I took two courses recommended by friends who assured me that each was a "gut" class, a sure "A" without much work. So I signed up for Music I and Speech I. Both turned out to be not only notably difficult but also life-changing.

Speech I was a public-speaking class. I was the only freshman in a class with mostly juniors and seniors, including several football players who were taking the class to raise their respective GPAs. The teacher, who had one glass eye, was irreverently called "the Cyclops" by several of the football players. Although I don't remember the teacher's name, the class itself was unforgettable. There were about fifteen to seventeen of us (mostly men) in the class, and we had to give a five- or six-minute speech every week: a speech to inform, to persuade, to amuse, and so forth. I was apprehensive each time, but I eventually learned how to speak easily in front of groups. Over the years parents, teachers, and friends have told me that public speaking is one of my greatest strengths as an educator. This skill began, without a doubt, in this class.

While I was catching up intellectually and realizing just how uneducated I had previously been, I became less social and lost all confidence with girls—or, as they were now called, women. I had two dates during my entire freshman year. I felt like Charlie Brown in the *Peanuts* comic strip—afraid to approach the cute redhead in the class. At that time the ratio of the sexes at Stanford was skewed—there were about five male students for every female student—but I'm not offering that fact to explain my lack of a social life. I also lost interest in sports: I went to one football game during my freshman year and maybe one more during the next few years. I remember sitting in the library on a Saturday afternoon, hearing the cheering from the stadium and feeling no regret at not being there. I began for the first time to pay attention to current events such as Martin Luther King Jr.'s rise to prominence, the bus boycotts in Montgomery, Alabama, and the resignations of Juan Peron and Winston Churchill. I read *The Quiet American*, Graham Greene's novel about America's involvement in Indochina (Vietnam was a place I had never heard of). Learning became all-absorbing. Well, almost all-absorbing.

During my sophomore year, my social life did pick up. In fact, I was "picked up" at a Wednesday evening candlelight service. For a while, it was my habit to study in an empty classroom in the inner quad until 9:30, then go over to the Stanford Church just to sit in quiet. Once, a girl approached me outside the church and asked me to walk her home. We began dating, and soon she introduced me to what Robert Penn Warren referred to as the "illicit sweetness of the flesh." She was wonderful, never making me feel clumsy or inexperienced—quite the contrary. I was in a vulnerable state, particularly after the football humiliation. Projecting sexuality and "experience," she was a fortunate bit of fate for me. I secretly enjoyed the teasing from my male friends about my new relationship. And I thoroughly enjoyed everything I "learned" from her.

My roommate, John Carswell, and I had both joined the Alpha Delta Phi fraternity, but after two weeks found ourselves in agreement about how impossible it was to study—or even sleep—in the frat house. Sophomores (pledges, like us) slept on the sophomore sleeping porch, and almost every night a drunken junior or a senior would come home late and decide to harass the pledges with firecrackers, water balloons, etc. Since I was now serious about my classes and studied until late each evening, I resented losing precious hours of sleep this way. John and I decided to move off campus. We rented an apartment and lived together for the next three years, forging a lifelong bond.

John, who had attended Andover, was light years ahead of me intellectually. He was particularly interested in literature, history, and philosophy, and I learned from him in countless ways. Sometimes we took courses together and would often talk into the wee hours while listening to classical music.

During my sophomore year, I became worried about Jon Harris, who seemed depressed. One morning, I went by his dorm room to walk to class with him and found him packing! "What the hell are you doing?" I asked.

"I'm leaving," he said. "I can't stand this place." While I was excited by Stanford, Jon felt just the opposite. He found his courses and his classmates equally superficial and couldn't seem to find a social circle.

"Where are you going?" I asked.

"Otto, my boy," he replied, using one of my high school football nicknames, "I am going to go around the world." I wouldn't see Jon again until spring quarter of my senior year.

with my college roomie John Carswell
in front of the Alpha Delta Phi house, Stanford

In addition to taking classes in European and U.S. history in my sophomore year, it was a fortuitous time to take a class in Russian history as well. This was the year, 1956, that Nikita Khrushchev denounced Stalin at the twentieth Communist Party Congress in Moscow, beginning the new era of "de-Stalinization" in the U.S.S.R. and Eastern Europe. It was also an eventful year to begin my study of American history. Eisenhower and Nixon had been re-elected, and Southern congressmen were calling upon states to resist "by all lawful means the Supreme Court ruling against segregation in the public schools." This ruling was, of course, the landmark 1954 *Brown v. Board of Education* decision. I idly wondered why no one in my family, or no teacher at my high school, had ever mentioned this momentous ruling. From the vantage point of today, I realize that my milieu was so insular, so "white-only," that the immorality of the segregated education of black children simply didn't register on anyone's consciousness.

Through some quirk in the Stanford distribution requirements and a mistake in the registrar's office, I found that I didn't have to take any math or foreign language courses; thus, I had virtually no restrictions on my choice of courses. I sampled a variety of courses as if I were a child in a candy store. Sociology I with Professor William M. "Bud" McCord introduced me to an entirely new domain. We read writers I had never heard of: Thorstein Veblen, Karl Marx, Max Weber, R.H. Tawney, Max Lerner, William Whyte, David Riesman, C. Wright Mills, and Vance Packard.

Wallace Stegner's class, Twentieth Century American Fiction, exposed me to Theodore Dreiser, Edith Wharton, John Dos Passos, Sherwood Anderson, Sinclair Lewis, F. Scott Fitzgerald, Ernest Hemingway, William Faulkner, Thomas Wolfe, and Robert Penn Warren. Encountering them I felt, as Keats had, like "Some watcher of the skies / When a new planet swims into his ken."

After studying excerpts from Veblen in McCord's Sociology class and now reading the brilliant mini-biography of Veblen by Don Passos within his U.S.A. trilogy, I was inspired to read the complete *Theory of the Leisure Class* and found myself laughing out loud at Veblen's skewering of upper-class pretentiousness. I immediately discerned "pecuniary emulation," "conspicuous consumption," and "conspicuous leisure" within my parents' country-club circle. Veblen argued that all social structures, being man-made, could be revised or even undone if people just noticed how silly and unfair most conventional forms of behavior were. I agree that social structures determine our destiny far more than does any natural endowment. To wit, here I was, culturally semi-illiterate, possessing an average intellect, studying at Stanford University. I was there only because I was white, from the lower echelons of the upper class, and had come from a private school with a father who could pull strings and pay full tuition. Had I been born black in East St. Louis, I would no more be at Stanford than on the third moon of Jupiter. Somehow this situation seemed unfair to me. While comically exposing the fatuity of social distinctions, Veblen also drove home a deeper truth.

I also found myself comprehending Theodore Dreiser's anguish over the plight of the poor and downtrodden, though I disagreed with his fundamental conclusion. As Alfred Kazin wrote in *On Native Grounds*: "Where other novelists of his time saw the evils of capitalism in terms of political or economic causation, Dreiser saw only the hand of fate." At this point in my education, I agreed with the "other novelists"; I saw not fatalistic but political and economic causes of social injustice.

Reading *The Great Gatsby* and Sinclair Lewis's *Babbitt* back to back led to yet another revelation. The pathos and ultimate hollowness of Jay Gatsby's dream of success alongside the sad, vulgar boorishness of George Babbitt, a member of H.L. Mencken's "booboisie," was a fruitful juxtaposition of novelistic visions, but it also made me look at my own background from a new perspective. *The Great Gatsby* showed my father's pursuit of his own domestic vision as a California version of West Egg, that nirvana that lay at the other side of the tracks if one simply worked hard enough. Jay Gatsby's boyhood schedule, reading like a list of Ben Franklin's maxims for success ("study electricity . . . work . . . practice elocution and how to attain it . . . read one improving book or magazine per week"), held the mirror up to my own father and his countless "to-do" lists. Gatsby mirrored not only my father's work ethic but his idea of the meaning of financial success as well. For Gatsby it was West Egg with its glitzy parties and Daisy, his goddess; for my father it was 310 North Carmelina Avenue in Brentwood, the exclusive Bel-Air Bay Club, and Ruthie—my mother—the beauty queen of Northwestern whom he married but lost to divorce after twenty-five years of pursuing his dream while neglecting his primary relationship.

In Stegner's American Fiction class, I became more alive to the nuances of language and the tragic struggles of writers to illuminate their own inner conflicts and, perhaps more importantly, to give their readers a more enlightened view of human affairs. I came to see heroism in a new way: not just as overcoming physical obstacles, as in war or sports, but also as laboring long hours to produce a good line of verse or a penetrating paragraph of prose. My new heroes were Dreiser, struggling with little educational preparation; Thomas Wolfe, furiously trying to write down "everything"—writing even on bathroom walls when he couldn't find paper; and Sherwood Anderson, sacrificing everything to capture the voices of lonely, depressed people.

From the time I was about twelve, I had enjoyed popular music (George Shearing, Ella Fitzgerald, and others) and musicals (*South Pacific*, *The Desert Song*, *Show Boat*). I had even enjoyed some classical music (for example, Rachmaninoff's Piano Concerto No. 2, which I first heard in a sappy movie with Elizabeth Taylor), though I had no knowledge about it. So I signed up for Music I—a music history class that introduced me to not only the range of composers from Bach to Bartok but also to theory, form, structure, and themes. I acquired a whole new vocabulary. I followed up Music I with a class in music theory, private piano lessons, then two more remarkable music history classes: The Concerto and The Symphony, both taught by Sandor Salgo, a Hungarian conductor, a former student of Bartok, and a warm, generous man. As soon as he would mention a piece such as Beethoven's "Eroica" or Brahms's Piano Concerto No. 2, or make a listening assignment, I would immediately drive into Palo Alto and buy the record, which John Carswell and I would then listen to over and over again. Salgo explicated one piece after another. Sonata form, rondo, theme and variations, prelude and fugue, passacaglia—Salgo's explanations of musical terms came almost too fast to absorb.

Sociology with McCord, American Fiction with Stegner, Music with Salgo— all of these, along with Daniel Smith's Western Civ., would have been quite enough to make for a rich college experience. Soon, however, I was to fall under the spell of perhaps my most profound influence, history professor Otis Pease.

I signed up for Twentieth Century U.S. History with Otis Pease in the spring of 1957. The textbook was *American Epoch* by Arthur S. Link. I still have the book and open it from time to time, not just for information but as a sort of pilgrimage to an important shrine. It reminds me of a course I attended with growing excitement as the year progressed. Otis Pease had a short, Ivy League crew cut, he often wore gray suits with conservative ties, and as he stood erect at his lectern, he looked almost as square and undramatic as the lectern itself. Gradually, I found that his lectures were pure gold. He was able to create a sense of drama merely by subtle inflections of his voice. His class on the Civil War was legendary among Stanford students, and when he lectured on the Battle of Gettysburg, the hall overflowed; many students who weren't even enrolled came to hear him. He would set the scene, and in almost whispered tones lead up to Pickett's Charge, which he then dramatized by reading from Steven Vincent Benet's "John Brown's Body."

I knew I was in the presence of a brilliant mind presenting meticulously crafted material. As I had done in Daniel Smith's class earlier, I wrote down the names of all the books Pease recommended and immediately bought or ordered them. My entire allowance from my father went into books, most of which I still have on my shelves. They are my companions to this day. I took every class taught by Otis Pease that I could: Twentieth Century U.S. History, The Civil War and Reconstruction, The Age of Big Business. Then I mustered up the courage to ask him whether I could undertake a three-quarter independent-study program under his direction. To my surprise, he agreed, and we selected "The Liberal Tradition in American History" as the general topic, using Louis Hartz's book by the same title as an initial guide. I was intimidated at the prospect of meeting with him alone to present weekly mini-essays and to engage him in conversation, but hell, I had survived Daniel Smith, so perhaps I could do this as well.

CHAPTER 14

Stanford Continued, 1957–1958: The Liberal Tradition Unveiled

Instead of recapturing our past,
we have got to transcend it.

—Louis Hartz,
The Liberal Tradition in America

I **FIRST LEARNED WHAT THE** word "liberal" meant in 1957, when I began a full-year exploration of its history, evolution, and current meaning with Otis Pease. Liberal was, and is, for me an honorable word. It describes the rich, profound thoughts and dreams of thinking men and women. The liberal tradition in America, which dates back to Jefferson, includes figures such as William James, John Dewey, Charles Beard, Ida Tarbell, Louis Brandeis, Theodore Roosevelt, and Woodrow Wilson, to name but a few of its leading lights. Now the word is denigrated by lightweight right-wing popularizers of "thought." I have no grandiose illusions that I can restore the word to its proper stature, but I can at least describe my own bond with it and say why I love what it represents.

My love affair with liberal thought may have begun when I first read Eric Goldman's *Rendezvous with Destiny*, a book Otis Pease recommended in his Twentieth Century American History class. From the first page, I was enthralled. Here was social, intellectual, and political history all woven into a lively drama of fascinating characters who collided and cooperated with each other. As Fred Allen once said of another writer, I believe was true of Goldman: "He writes so well he makes me feel like putting my quill back in the goose."

Goldman began by discussing an 1870s America "in which both the hopelessly poor and the overwhelmingly rich were *limited* in numbers," and the chief evil of the day was "the alliance between industrialists." This disreputable alliance eventuated in what Lyman Trumbull called in 1871 an "age of reform" (the title of a wonderful book by Richard Hofstadter, who became another one of my intellectual heroes).

I had watched my father become successful by hard work, initiative, and ingenuity—all solid American values. But I had also observed that he was never discriminated against. His skin color, his ethnicity, his family background, even the part of the country he was from (Iowa) were never impediments to his ambition. Furthermore, I realized, he was an exceptional man. He had an "exceptional" ability to make money. Not everyone does. It seemed appropriate to me that the American economy should reward exceptional men such as my father—and, on a grander scale, men like John D. Rockefeller or Jay Gould. However, I also believed it should not permit grossly disproportionate wealth, whereby the success of the few dictated that many would be unable to escape the underclass. Simple fairness suggested that creative people should be allowed some of the fruits of their labor but not the entire tree. Unable to accept an exclusively economic theory of history, I looked forward to each of my tutorials with Professor Pease as I found myself becoming increasingly aware of the complexities, inequities, and disparate versions of American history. I learned, for example, that many titans of industry were not in the mold of Rockefeller or Gould. Henry Ford paid his workers a living wage, if only so they could buy his cars, and Andrew Carnegie, with his endowment of libraries and institutions of learning across the land, was an exemplary philanthropist.

We examined the debate between the Social Darwinists and the Social Gospel Movement and compared the notions of social determination to social reform as well as unlimited capital accumulation with progressive taxation. I found myself baffled by the lengths to which well-educated people would go to rationalize greed, inequality, and therefore poverty. Those who demolished these self-interested rationalizations were my heroes: Veblen, Henry George, Clarence Darrow, Richard Ely, and Oliver Wendell Holmes Jr.

My year-long "Liberal Tradition in American History" independent study project with Otis Pease was having an enormous impact on me. It was the intellectual equivalent of an earthquake. I was learning to put my life, my background, and my family history into a larger context. I now had a framework within which I could see the implicit and not-so-subtle forms of anti-Semitism or racism of my "class," my race, and my parents' social milieu. Whether or not it is accurate to say "the unexamined life is not worth living," I came to believe that the unexamined life imprisons an individual in his or her own ignorance.

I had attended a private high school that had one or two Jews, one Mexican (a wealthy exchange student whose father was a major landowner), no Asians, and no blacks—not a single one. I suppose the social stratification was so strong that not only would none of "those people" have been accepted into the school, none would have even considered applying. Even Stanford in the 1950s was not exactly a hotbed of multiculturalism. Few of my classes had black students, and few of my reading lists included works by blacks, Asians, Latinos, or women.

What is difficult to recapture in words is the sheer drama of ideas that were coming to life for me. Not just ideas in cloudy vagaries but ideas connected to life itself and magically presented in books. I can almost recall the sensation of holding some of these books for the first time, and their covers are indelibly emblazoned in my memory: books such as Herbert J. Muller's *The Uses of the Past*, Crane Brinton's *The Shaping of Modern Thought*, Jacques Barzun's *Darwin, Marx, Wagner*, and Herbert Butterfield's *Napoleon*. Somehow just holding these books and then folding sections of the pages back so the paperback spine would not break created a delicious prelude to actually beginning the reading. And for a newcomer to each idea, each historical figure and period, each conflict of ideas and factions, each of these introductions was a wild play performed upon a stage so immense that I was overcome with excitement and a growing awareness of my own ignorance and the lifetime of attacking that ignorance that lay ahead.

My heroes were no longer just Joe DiMaggio and Otto Graham, but thinkers such as Morton White, Thorstein Veblen, Edmund Wilson, Eric Goldman, and Alfred Kazin. Their books sit on my shelves to this day—not just as monuments of my own past, but as friends, mentors, and symbols of the worlds they opened up to me.

As I learned more, I began to see how society absorbed historical events and ideas in unconscious, unexamined ways. While reading *Social Darwinism in American Thought* (another book by Richard Hofstadter) and learning about conservatism in general, I recognized that conservatism was the outlook of men who saw property rights as supreme and who believed that these rights were rooted in biological, psychological, or even moral laws. As I read these absurd arguments, it struck me that they were the underlying assumptions of my parents' social circle. I loved my parents and liked many of their friends, but their attitudes toward social justice disturbed me greatly. It was a disturbance I have wrestled with ever since.

Now that I am a school administrator, I sympathize with parents who fear that education will cause their children to reject parental values. All I can say to them is "Yes, I understand; it has been known to happen" (and, I silently add, "to me").

For all of its pseudoscientific trappings, conservative Darwinism seemed wrong-headed to me. An environment that had been made by human beings could be changed by human beings. Disparities of wealth were not immutable laws; conservative Darwinism had created, as Goldman argued, "a science of selfishness." I came to believe in reform—not at some future time, but in the present. Eric Goldman concluded a discussion of Henry George with a sentence I never forgot: "Legislating a better environment, particularly a better economic environment, could bring about a better world and bring it about before unconscionable centuries." Goldman wrote this sentence almost fifty years ago, in the mid-twentieth century. As we move into a new century, his moral call to action seems all the more urgent, and our delays in ameliorating poverty in our country seem even more unconscionable to me.

Reform became a magic word for me. It meant to begin anew, to change things—as Tennyson wrote, "to seek a newer world." Goldman, Hofstadter, Morton White, and, of course, Otis Pease were the magicians to whom I apprenticed myself. Reform seemed to me a better avenue than revolution. From my first week at Stanford and my encounter with *Animal Farm* and *1984*, I came to believe that revolution generally replaces one set of tyrants with another: violence begets extremism, rather than encouraging an inclusive concern for the human rights of all. But reform, that was another matter. The ideas of the reformers at that time hit me like proverbial thunderbolts. Judge Ben Lindsey advocated rehabilitation for juvenile offenders—a new concept; John Peter Altgeld argued that poverty was the root cause of most crime, adult or juvenile. Clarence Darrow and Franz Boas argued that "culture was a cumulative evolutionary product, not a function of racial heredity," and David Graham Phillips argued that what was wrong with women was men—men "who insisted that a woman should be educated to be a doodle-wit." I listened to these ideas, and I decided that if men made things, men could change them. I was, however, still thinking in terms of men, and white men at that; Stanford did little to encourage notions of gender or racial equity in those days.

From these social reformers, my focus broadened to Reform Darwinism's legal impact. I discovered that "law" was and should be a constantly evolving set of ideas. Furthermore, I came to believe that the Constitution was basically an economic document reflecting the interests of its framers. Here a whole new set of reformist heroes were added to my intellectual Hall of Fame. Oliver Wendell Holmes Jr., for example, wrote that "the life of the law has not been logic: it has been experience," and Roscoe Pound insisted that the judge makes the actual law. Not only does the law continually evolve, he believed, but it was "the judge's duty consciously to shape law to the needs of the day."

After Roscoe Pound, I read Louis Brandeis, Frederick Jackson Turner, Algie M. Simons, and then J. Allen Smith's *The Spirit of American Government*—a sadly neglected book. "The Constitution," Smith maintained, "was an artificial creation . . . of a minority of large property owners intensely concerned with preventing a majority of have-nots from getting control of the government." He contended that the framers were profit-minded and little else. In words shockingly reminiscent of government critics in the 1990s, Smith wrote in 1907 that "the active cause of corruption . . . is to be found in the selfishness and greed of those who are the recognized leaders in commercial and industrial affairs." In 1957, during the quiet, peaceful days of the Eisenhower era, a sleepy time on the Stanford campus interrupted only by the noise of an occasional panty raid, Smith was a surprise. I was in for an even bigger shock with my next assigned reading: *An Economic Interpretation of the Constitution*, by Charles Beard.

If Smith was a jolt, Beard was a full-scale shock. Not only was the Constitution not a sacred text, Beard argued, it was clearly a partisan, elitist apologia of self-interested monied groups. In a sober, well-documented, and non-inflammatory tome, Beard pointed out that the large mass of propertyless Americans had been excluded from the framing of the Constitution, which had been ratified by a vote of no more than one-sixth of the adult male population. What I was learning in my own limited way was that whatever social institutions existed at any one time reflected the interests of those in power and were therefore not sacred and immutable. Change for the greater good of greater numbers of people was indeed possible.

One day, in the spring of my junior year, during a boring lecture, I began daydreaming and doodling. When the class ended, I emerged from my reverie and realized that I had filled three pages with an outline of a high school curriculum. My own high school years had been a wasteland with one boring, intellectually impoverished class after another. Yet, within two weeks of attending Stanford, Jon Harris and Daniel Smith had transformed me. I realized I had been "ready" to learn in high school, but compelling ideas just hadn't been presented to me. Ideas, themes and conflicts, the ongoing drama of human history had been absent from my high school. I think I would have been willing to eat if only I had been fed. I had gone off to college with vague notions of going to law school someday (my dad had said, "It's great preparation for business"), then going into the restaurant and real estate business with my dad. That day I looked at my doodled "curriculum" and thought to myself, "My God, perhaps you should go into education." Later that week, I wrote my dad a letter, telling him of my new ideas. The following excerpts convey the gist and proved to chart what became my professional journey, fairly accurately.

Dear Dad,

For a long while now, I've been meaning to tell you many things—what I think about, want to do in life, etc. . . . but for an equally long time, such thoughts have been so confused and indescribable that I've been unable to make any attempt to express them to you.

I'm sure you have wondered on many occasions what has run through your son's mind. I hardly know where to begin—Stanford has been such a period of awakening . . . (I even now find that I enjoy reading the front page more than the sports page). At any rate, I am now reasonably sure I want to look deeply into education. I find myself incensed over the educational waste my four years at Harvard [prep. school] were—not that Harvard was not a wonderful experience, but that such unlimited opportunities to have my mind developed were wasted. I could spend this whole letter and then some discussing what is wrong with education in America—anyway the Sputnik shock seems to be making many people realize that our educational system is not so efficient. But the failure does not lie only in Math and Science; it lies also in the lack of decent liberal arts courses and the general anti-intellectual attitudes of the schools. Harvard is supposedly superior to most California schools, yet not once at Harvard was I inspired or required to ask myself "What is the meaning of life?" . . . "Why am I here on Earth, and what is my relation to my fellow man?" These are questions which I feel every man must answer to give his life any meaning. I am not sure that there is any one meaning or answer, but it seems that every man must come to some decision regarding these fundamental questions. And, once such a decision is reached, he must then live his life in an all-out, total effort at fulfilling the goals he has set for himself. Here, I think, lies the worth of any man . . . not so much what he decides as how honestly and determinedly he strives to achieve his goals. Also, I think every man has an obligation to do his part, be it large or small, in improving the lot of his fellow man. Perhaps my part lies in education, although I don't want to teach all my life, I would like to teach for a few years though . . .

Nancy Dwyer sent me an article the other day about a young man who started an independent school of his own in Redlands. I'm anxious to talk to this man, for the school sounds as though it really gives the students a fine education . . . math, science, foreign languages in first grade, etc. . . . not a school for gifted students but for kids of just good intelligence, with a good balance of social activities. I mention this because the thought of building a school someday myself is with me every day. I constantly dream of building and leading a school where students are encouraged and helped to: seek the meaning of life, read and discuss the world's great literature and music, to speak a foreign language and not just memorize vocabulary words which will be forgotten in a few years' time, to have a knowledge of current events, . . . and so on into the night. At any rate, this is perhaps my greatest dream and has been increasingly so for the last two years. I have also thought that perhaps someday you and I might work together on such a project . . .

Despite my criticism of the American system of education, I am convinced that America is a wonderful land . . . that men have the opportunity to make limitless accomplishments and to express themselves as they so choose is a privilege not known to many. (My father's life is a wonderful example and tribute to the American ideal.) And I think that it is a land and govt. worth devoting oneself to perpetuating. And as I have said, I think that I may possibly do my part in serving this country in the field of education. At any rate, I do very much want to give it a try. I'd better wind this up for now, as I have a political science test tomorrow . . .

Please take care of yourself. I could not bear anything happening to you.

With love,

Paul

Almost instantly I received his blessing—"You know, son, whatever your heart tells you to do is what you should do"—and I began looking at my courses with a different perspective: how would I teach this book or this concept someday? It added a new dimension to learning.

After a summer of travel to Europe, I spent a few weeks with my family and began to notice a growing tension between my parents. I was also worried about my father, who seemed to be working extraordinarily long hours and experiencing severe business problems. Soon, however, it was time to pack to return to Stanford for my senior year.

CHAPTER 15

Senior Year at Stanford: Farewell to Palo Alto

Man's reason can solve most of his problems if given a chance . . .

—Otis Pease (1962)

ARRIVING BACK AT STANFORD IN August of 1958, though deeply worried about my dad, I was also eager to see my roomie, John Carswell, and resume my independent study program. I wasn't yet concerned about what to do after graduation, although very quickly I observed classmates beginning to experience angst over what to do next. I also noticed senior girls becoming more attentive as a rash of pinnings (wearing a guy's fraternity pin—a sort of pre-engagement engagement) broke out. For me, however, classes were still so exciting that they absorbed most of my thought. Going into education now seemed to be a given.

As I continued my independent study program with Otis Pease, we moved from the legal-reform thinking of Beard to reform philosophers, William James and John Dewey. According to Eric Goldman, James believed that "both the mind and the material things it thought about were constantly evolving, and evolving in relation to each other." This statement seems obvious, but it has had monumental manifestations in the world. Certainly for an aspiring educator dreaming of someday starting a school, this was an encouraging thought.

Reading John Dewey further confirmed my reform ideals. I was struck primarily by Dewey's notion that "ideas could and should change to give men what they sought." I found conservatism an inadequate approach to social problems because of its insistence that evolution stopped at the present, leaving in place whatever privileges the power structure was enjoying. The environment conservatives championed was one in which the well-being of the majority of human beings was sacrificed for the benefit of the few. This outlook did not seem to me the end stage of evolution; it seemed pure and simple selfishness. It seemed grossly unfair.

Life wasn't just books and lectures, and one night at Stanford seems worth recalling just for the hell of it—or perhaps just for the ego of it. After my freshman football debacle, I had pretty much given up sports, except for shooting baskets several times a week as relaxation—almost a meditative practice. In my senior year, I did join our fraternity team to compete in the fraternity intramural league. Most teams were composed of frustrated former high school stars, so the league was feisty and intense. My fraternity, Alpha Delta Phi, was not especially a "jock house," and we lost more than we won. This particular night, we had to play the Delts, distinctly an athletic house. They didn't take us too seriously. Somehow we managed to keep the score close, although they remained arrogant and seemingly unconcerned with the score. Finally, with the game almost over, I called a timeout. "Hey, we're down by one point," I said. "Let's do it." We went back out on the court, and I took the inbound pass. With three seconds left, I launched a jump shot that to my delight hit "nothing but net." We won! However, none of the Delts shook hands or even said a word; they simply disappeared into the night. My own teammates, who seemed equally oblivious to the fact that my shot had won the game, also disappeared into the night. I was left standing virtually alone in the gym, feeling baffled, let down, even dazed. What the hell was going on? Finally, my girlfriend came down from the bleachers and said, "Good shot; who won?"

I said, "My last shot won the game." She smiled and kissed me, a nice, long kiss. It was a special moment. My one athletic triumph at Stanford was at least acknowledged by someone.

During this time, I discovered an intellectual hero whose views helped explain the despotism of a Stalin, a Tito, or a Joe McCarthy, as well as the failures of a Djilas, a William Jennings Bryan, or a Eugene Debs to attract a sizable popular following. Both Russian and American utopian socialist philosophies took as their premise the inherent intelligence and rationalism of man, the essential goodness and unselfishness of human beings, and the ultimate perfectibility of society, i.e., that it was possible to achieve "heaven on earth." In America these views, sometimes referred to as "naïve liberalism," were fueled in part by the Social Gospel Movement, which had begun in the 1880s under the intellectual leadership of Walter Rauschenbusch and which was given a humanistic and social rationale by John Dewey and others. My other new intellectual hero, who disdained sentimental optimism, was Reinhold Niebuhr, whose writings Otis Pease assigned me. Niebuhr was sympathetic to the Social Gospel Movement early in his career but gradually came to see that "the Kingdom of God would never be fully realized on earth," that no acts could escape the stain of self-interest, and that "what is in history is always partial to specific interests and tainted by sin."

In his book *The Children of Light and the Children of Darkness*, Niebuhr passionately defended democracy but did not rationalize away its unbridled greed and rampant individualism. Instead, he argued, "man's capacity for justice makes democracy possible; but man's inclination to injustice makes democracy necessary." Consequently, Niebuhr recommended an expansion of true democracy. He argued that "if men are inclined to deal unjustly with their fellows, the possession of power only aggravates this inclination. That is why irresponsible and uncontrolled power is the greatest source of injustice." Niebuhr explained how injustice can occur in so-called democracies as well as in totalitarian forms of government. Thus, in a curious way, I found both Djilas and Niebuhr to be prophets who formulated a more comprehensive view of the world than most American political leaders were offering. Djilas pointed out that a new class of tyrants had simply replaced the old ones. Niebuhr went beyond Djilas to point out that "even if one class were able to eliminate all other classes, which is hardly probable, it would require some social grace and moral dynamic to preserve harmony between the various national groups by which this vast mass would be organized and into which it would disintegrate."

While America was a freer and more open society than Russia and the other Iron Curtain countries, it, too, was in urgent need of reform. In 1958–59, I believed we were foolishly preparing for war against a nation we regarded as evil incarnate rather than acknowledging our own national problems and spending the funds necessary to ameliorate injustices within our own borders. Expressing these views in the 1950s and 1960s was, at best, akin to belching at a church social and, at worst, nearly treasonable. I couldn't help myself; I didn't see communism as the world threat our leaders kept insisting it was. In hindsight, I can at least take some satisfaction in believing that my assessment was for the most part accurate. However, self-satisfaction is not really the issue. The real issue is that salvation is not to be found either in nationalistic ideologies or in rampant individualism but in community, especially in communities that understand human limitation and celebrate global diversity. I also realized even more clearly the ironic fate of liberalism—in both the nineteenth and the twentieth centuries. The word *liberal* has close ties to the word *liberty*. To be a "liberal" had at one time in the eighteenth century (and in pre-revolutionary and colonial America) meant believing in the freedom of the individual, particularly an individual who had been deprived of certain rights by an oppressive government. America, after all, came into being in opposition to British oppression; therefore, we were determined to preserve the individual's right to determine his own life—particularly his economic fate. Early in American history, however, when class conflict emerged, liberals (Jeffersonians and Jacksonians) came to identify themselves primarily with yeomen, the farmers and mechanics and laborers in opposition to the "monied interests"—bankers, large landowners, speculators, and lawyers, those who could amass wealth without physical labor.

Initially, liberals feared government as a tool of the rich to perpetuate power. But gradually in the popular mind capitalism became synonymous with democracy. As materialism came to dominate American life, captains of industry gained more and more power, and liberals found that laissez-faire no longer served the cause of liberty. With the passage of time, a further late-twentieth-century shift has occurred, with big government having become the unholy partner of big business and the military. While conservatives still preach laissez-faire and still denounce the welfare state, at the same time they are happy enough to benefit from a "corporate welfare state" with subsidies, grants, deregulatory actions, tax breaks, and so forth. This marriage of business and government has led to the emasculation of the union movement, the trashing of the word *liberalism*, and the remarkably effective conflation of capitalism with democracy in the popular mind, all under the banner of "Americanism." The humorist Fran Lebowitz put it as succinctly as is humanly possible: "In the Soviet Union, capitalism triumphed over Communism; in this country, capitalism over democracy."

Today, schools seem to be the only place from which genuine reform can emanate. Only from educators willing to look closely at the widening gap between rich and poor—or the sacrifice of tomorrow's trees and seas for today's profits—can tomorrow's leaders emerge. We already have enough books about the reforms we need to revitalize America's soul; what we desperately need are leaders who can envision and show the way. Only a proper education will be able to prepare our youth for that task.

Meanwhile, back in 1958, another dramatic event was taking place in my life. My father's financial ascent, as impressive and rapid as it had been, came to an equally rapid and crashing halt. He had overextended himself by purchasing a string of restaurants from two scoundrels who misrepresented their books, sticking him with a huge tax liability. Several banks called in loans, and my father faced bankruptcy. While I was writing essays about "the liberal tradition," he was trying to stave off ruin by declaring Chapter 11 (all his assets were taken over by a creditor corporation that, in turn, ran the remaining assets into bankruptcy). During Christmas vacation that year my father told me that I was now on my own financially. I applied for loans and secured part-time jobs to pay for my other expenses. My father lived out his last twenty-five years by his wits and managed to maintain a house with a tennis court and swimming pool. My sister and I never quite figured out how he did it.

During the first quarter of my senior year, I began thinking of applying to graduate school. A friend said he was applying to Harvard for a PhD program in history and suggested I do so as well. I knew that my B average was not good enough to get me into the Harvard history department, and, besides, I had already decided to teach at the high school level. Perhaps, I thought, I should apply to the Graduate School of Education at Harvard. With several generous letters of recommendation, including one from Otis Pease, I applied to Harvard's Master of Arts in Teaching (MAT) program. To my great surprise, I was accepted for the fall of 1959 and was even granted a student loan.

**Graduation from Stanford,
June 1959**

CHAPTER 16

From Cambridge to the Black Horse Troop: 1959–1961

. . . And soon now we shall go out of the house
and go into the convulsion of the world, out of history
into history and the awful responsibility of time.

—Robert Penn Warren, *All the King's Men*

I ARRIVED IN CAMBRIDGE, MASSACHUSETTS, in September of 1959. I was housed in a dormitory appropriately and fortuitously named William James Hall. My roommate, Jerome Ginzburg—also from Stanford—was a brilliant student and stimulating conversationalist. We had coffee one day with a girl he was dating, and a friend of hers joined us. I found her attractive and later suggested to Jerry that we double-date sometime. "Oh, she wouldn't go out with a goy," he said.

My clueless Brentwood-Stanford WASP upbringing manifested itself as I asked, "What's a goy?"

"You, dummy," he replied, "you're a goy."

In addition to Jerry, a contingent of Stanford history majors had come to Harvard to study history and education, and several of us attributed our choice of history and our vocational aspirations directly to Otis Pease's influence. I had dinner once a week at the apartment of three young women, fellow Pease devotees from Stanford, and it was there, early in the fall, that I heard a tragic piece of news.

A visitor to the apartment had just come from Palo Alto, and I asked him whether he had seen our mutual friend Jon Harris recently. "Didn't you hear?" he asked.

"Hear what?" I said.

"Jon died in a motorcycle accident last summer." I was devastated. I got up, walked out the door in a daze, wandered around the streets of Cambridge for an hour or so, then went to my dorm room and wept.

I had last seen Jon a month before graduation, in May of 1959. He showed up at my door one day out of the blue. I hadn't heard from him since receiving a postcard from Bali a year or so before. He had completed his trip around the world and had finished up in Europe, where he bought a motorcycle. Returning to the United States, uncertain about what to do, he determined to discharge any military duties he might have to perform by enlisting in the Army and applying for the Army Language School in Monterey, California. We went out for pizza, several beers, and then a wild ride on his motorcycle through the hills above Palo Alto. At one point we tipped his bike over and rolled down a hill, falling over each other, giggling joyously. The next morning he came over to say goodbye; he would soon be off to Monterey. I never saw him again. He had driven off a cliff somewhere between Big Sur and Carmel. Years later I wrote a poem about Jon and his impact on my life.

A POSTCARD FROM BALI

Jon

decades have passed

and memories still surface

like dolphins breaching for air

i never wrote to your dad

he's probably dead now

mine is

i wanted to ask him for a picture

but you were gone

and that was that

i got the news in grad school

wandered Brattle street

drifted into a bar

poured down a few unhelpful beers

and returned to dinner

there was no one to talk to

you changed me
i remember meeting
in line freshman year
skinny, long neck, carrot hair
you asked me what i was reading
hell, Jon, i didn't read then
i was dumb as dough
but you gave me *Catcher*
selecting my first books
with a parent's care
you set me in motion
your prodding, ridicule
angered me into learning
so while you
Baudelaire in your hip pocket
dropped out, hopped a freighter
and traveled the world
i began to read
to learn about the written world
that world you knew so well
yet feared to join
i still read like a psalm
your postcard from Bali
the content long since memorized
now time has changed
the calendar useful only
to mark off children's birthdays
somehow for me
you are still a postcard away
i say your name and there you are
harassing me
determined to make a silk purse

when your body broke on the Big Sur rocks
was some muse released who gravitates
to jazz records with Kid Ory, George Lewis,
Louis Armstrong and all the creole crew?

or when someone with tragic sense picks up Unamuno
are you there applauding over his shoulder?
there were only a few who knew you
do we hold exclusive power to call
and spirit you back?

I dream, Jon, of two motorcycle rides
you and i, high,
flying through the Palo Alto countryside,
turning over, tumbling down the hill
ass over teakettle laughing
we were as close as wafer and wine
i can't pretend any premonitions
we simply said goodbye the next day
i never thought it would end there
when you and your bike were flying again
hurtling through the cold wind
to the rocks below
was it an accident, Jon?
while i think i know
i see a picture in slow motion reverse
see you tumbling back up the hill
laughing your way back.

The excitement I had felt at Stanford was even more intense at Harvard, with its three hundred years of tradition. At one point I was taking four classes and auditing three others, two of which I was finally forced to relinquish.

During the second semester I was required to do student teaching. I was supposed to observe my master teacher, Mr. M., for several weeks, submit a lesson plan, then gradually co-teach with him. I arrived on my first day at Somerville High School, found Mr. M. in the teachers' lounge, and introduced myself. "Oh, you're the bright guy from Harvard," he said. "Here's the key to Room 402—go up and teach a class on Jeffersonian democracy, will you? It begins in ten minutes. I have a meeting." I was so stunned I couldn't think of anything to say. He got up and left, and I wandered the halls searching for Room 402. I racked my brains to think of a few things I could say about Thomas Jefferson. Somerville High, located in a blue-collar community adjacent to Cambridge, was then divided into four categories of students: college prep (about 10 percent of the students); general (about

30 percent, slotted into pre-white-collar vocational courses); commercial (about 30 percent, taking other types of vocational classes); and retail (a euphemism for the weakest students). Needless to say, I was appalled by these labels—and what in hell did "retail" even mean as a designation for a weak student, exactly?

I arrived at Room 402 as nervous as I have ever been. Upon opening the door, I found myself looking at a class of twenty-seven senior *retail girls!* They took one look at me, a twenty-three-year-old preppie in a tie and corduroy jacket, and began squealing and giggling wildly. Some of them, quite worldly-wise, looked me up and down in a way that must have caused me to blush at least six shades of crimson. Spurred on by my shyness and inexperience, they proceeded to tease me unmercifully. I tried to teach them something about Jefferson, but it was a forty-five-minute nightmare. When I got back to Harvard I had the good sense to discuss my ordeal with my student-teaching advisor, who arranged a meeting with Mr. M. and got the student-teaching process back on track. As one might imagine, Mr. M. didn't appreciate being taken to task and never did treat me very well, though at the end he softened a bit and even managed to thank me.

I enjoyed preparing occasional lessons for my Somerville teaching, but I enjoyed even more taking classes from Arthur Schlesinger Jr., Leon Edel (The Modern Novel), Donald Oliver (Methods of Teaching History), and George Buttrick (Contemporary Theology). In Schlesinger's class I was able to continue my study of the meaning of liberalism in American history. Given his work on FDR and the New Deal (a four-volume study of the Age of Roosevelt), I was encouraged to read more about men such as John Maynard Keynes, Harry Hopkins, Raymond Moley, and Felix Frankfurter, as well as the "big government" organizations known by their acronyms: the NRA, the WPA, and the CCC. In one lecture Schlesinger opined that big business in America should erect a monument to FDR with the inscription "He saved capitalism." Several students hissed, but Schlesinger simply smiled a wry smile. (I repeated the story one Friday night that year while visiting the house of a friend whose father was an arch-conservative businessman. He got up from the dinner table, stormed into his bedroom, and began packing a valise to go to his yacht for the weekend. It took his wife a half hour to calm him down.) Schlesinger's theories resonated with me. I began to see that the central tension throughout American history has come from the conflict between individual freedom and collective security. The Depression had been the result of individual economic freedom run wild. FDR had simply tried to restore collective security without fundamentally altering the systems that enabled individuals to pursue their private goals. Furthermore, one might ask, if government doesn't look out for the poor and disenfranchised, who will? It is a question I have repeatedly asked my students, colleagues, and conservative acquaintances for the past fifty-plus years, and I have yet to hear of a reasonable alternative.

Father William Scott Chalmers, my high school headmaster at Harvard School, came to visit me in Boston in January of 1960 and offered me a full-time position teaching history at my old high school. I accepted. So when various recruiters from schools all over America descended upon the Harvard Graduate School of Education in the spring, I didn't attend any interviews, since I thought I already had a job. Then in May—coincidentally about one week before my draft board was to meet—I received a letter from Father Chalmers: He was terribly sorry, but he would have to withdraw the offer, as the Board of Trustees had voted not to expand the faculty for the next year. He would, however, have a job the following year, he wrote. I did not know at the time that this was a complete fabrication—his board didn't vote on such matters; he had simply decided to offer the job to someone else. (That someone else, I discovered three years later, was my close friend Nat Reynolds, who had been in an MA program at Johns Hopkins but decided to return to Los Angeles. Chalmers offered him the job he had earlier promised me.) When I first received Chalmers's letter, I was dumbfounded and told the dire news to my Harvard classmate and new friend Jack O'Donnell, who said he had been hired by the Culver Military Academy in Indiana and was sure it needed another English teacher. "But I'm a history teacher," I protested. "Oh, hell," he said, "just tell them you'll teach English; they'll be delighted to get another young guy from Harvard." Which is how I got started teaching English.

Culver Military Academy is situated at one end of Lake Maxinkuckee, in the northern part of Indiana. The academy, a boarding school with eight hundred students, has a gorgeous campus that many colleges would envy. Another noted feature of the academy is its famous Black Horse Troop, a cavalry unit of about two hundred black horses. Students wore uniforms, and their military bearing and courtesy were a welcome contrast to the vibrant but raucous behavior of my Somerville High "retail girls." At Culver I taught four English classes (two ninth-grade and two tenth-grade) and one eleventh-grade U.S. history class. To my surprise, I found that I enjoyed teaching English more than history. I had "prepared" to be an English teacher by taking two classes at UCLA in the summer of 1960—both, Shakespeare and modern poetry, taught by Reginald Mutter, an excellent visiting professor from England.

My Culver salary was $3,900, which included room and board. I brought with me a debt to Harvard University of more than $2,000 but managed to pay it back within the next nine months—there was simply nothing to spend it on. Culver, Indiana, was an isolated place and a lonely one for a young bachelor.

But the eighteen-member English department was superb, and I contented myself with attaching myself to several faculty, persistently asking questions about how to teach this or that. My fellow teachers were patient and helpful. One day, my colleague Norm Wagner gave me a copy of Robert Penn Warren's *All the King's Men*. I started reading it one Saturday morning, and except for sandwiches and bathroom visits, I read it straight through until midnight Sunday. The final line of the book was indelibly imprinted on my mind: "Soon now we shall go out of the house and go into the convulsion of the world, out of history into history and the awful responsibility of time." Next I read Warren's *World Enough and Time*. I became a lifelong Robert Penn Warren devotee.

In my enthusiasm I assigned *All the King's Men* to my tenth-grade classes. It was probably too hard a novel for this grade level, but somehow I "sold" it. I remember one student coming up to me on a Monday morning, all breathless and excited. He had finished the novel over the weekend; he just couldn't put it down. "It was great, thank you for assigning it—gee—wow—what a book!" he said. This and similar experiences validated me in my decision to be a teacher. When all is going well, there is a "high" that comes during classroom teaching. It doesn't happen every day, but it happens to good teachers often enough to keep them fueled for months at a time. During this time, I was so excited and overprepared each day that I was a good teacher almost from the very start.

Sometime during the winter I wrote Father Chalmers and reaffirmed my desire to return to Los Angeles and teach at my old high school. He wrote back and, for the second time, offered me a job. This time his offer stood, and in June of 1961 I returned to Los Angeles.

CHAPTER 17

Harvard School, 1961–1965:
The Moderate as Radical

We shall never be again
as we were.

—Henry James

Six years after having graduated from Harvard School, I was back. I was actually splitting a position with Jack O'Donnell, with whom I had become good friends as we taught together at Culver Military Academy the previous year. This year, we would both be teaching two classes at Harvard School while attending graduate school at USC.

Returning to Harvard School felt like coming home. It ultimately would prove to be a sometimes difficult seven-year relationship. Some challenges arose right away: I—actually Jack and I—came under fire almost immediately from some "conservative" parents and then from the John Birch Society. Some of our students had begun challenging their parents with "new ideas" on issues such as capital punishment, the unequal distribution of wealth in America, gun control, and civil rights. While I was teaching traditional writers such as Shakespeare, Dickens, George Eliot, and Thomas Hardy, I was also asking my students to read and write essays about contemporary issues. The headmaster, Father Chalmers, called me into his office and asked me whether I was teaching English or politics. When I explained my approach, he seemed temporarily satisfied.

Not long after that, Jack and I were summoned to the law office of a Harvard School trustee. His Beverly Hills office was appointed with sets of pristine leather-bound books, neatly hung degrees and paintings of English hunting scenes, and huge leather chairs facing an immense mahogany desk. No sooner had we seated ourselves than he launched his attack on us. Weren't we patriots? Didn't we value capitalism and Americanism? Over the course of about ten minutes, he spoke louder and louder, telling us how he had worked his way up from obscure beginnings to his current eminence. Who were we—pissant intellectuals—to challenge the American way? Finally, we looked at each other—Jack was red in the face—and I stood up and said, "This is just about enough." Before I could say more, he interrupted me and, in a totally different tone, told us that while he differed with our opinions, he would defend with his life our right to state them. He told us calmly that he realized we were young and idealistic, but perhaps we should be just a little more circumspect in the expression of our ideas. We took our leave of him feeling both angry and puzzled.

Soon we were presented with a list of accusations against us that, as I discovered, a chapter of the John Birch Society had circulated and discussed at one of its meetings. The list contained pretty silly stuff. One complaint, for example, concerned something I had supposedly written, which was actually a quotation from Karl Marx, and I had asked my seniors to analyze. The Birchers had simply eliminated Marx's name from the assignment so that it looked as if the quotation came from me. One charge did disturb me, however: that I was encouraging students to disagree with and disrespect their parents' views. This was not my conscious goal, but I wondered, was I really doing this indirectly? From then on, when expressing my views to students, I always prefaced my remarks by reminding students that I have my own biases, that they should think for themselves and not accept any point of view just because a teacher says it is so. I began all my remarks by saying, "It seems to me . . ."

In 1995, I received a letter from a student I taught during those turbulent 1960s. It came from out of the blue—I hadn't heard from, or of, its author for more than thirty years. He commented how impressed he had been by my always saying, "It seems to me . . ." The phrase, somehow, inspired his trust.

January 9, 1995
Dear Paul, yes, "Paul" would be O.K. now I think,

I have been meaning to write this for thirty years so I guess I better do it before one of us gets hit by a truck . . . or a "drive by." I'm certain that you are "The Teacher" for many people, but I wanted to add my deepest if belated gratitude to the long line.

"IT SEEMS TO ME." You always used to say that. "IT SEEMS TO ME." It was the greatest phrase in the world! When I have the wit to remember I try to use it like you did; honestly, simply, a natural part of the package. Four words that change everything, especially when you're young and you haven't a clue who you are. What a wonderful gift! That magical, life affirming "IT SEEMS TO ME" used to just knock me out. Still does. Few days pass where the phrase doesn't rein me in, center me, RE-MIND me. You LED us to think, set up the proper circumstances and let it happen, AND you made it O.K. NOT TO KNOW. Thank you forever.

STEPHEN WHITE, CLASS OF '65

One incident at Harvard School I would like very much to forget. Jack O'Donnell was dismissed at the end of our first year of teaching there. Father Chalmers told me that there was room for only one of us to stay. But I had already had experience with his tendency to prevaricate, and deep down I knew that Jack was the sacrificial lamb being offered up to the "John Birch" altar of some of the board members who couldn't tolerate two young radicals on the faculty. In hindsight, I wish I had also quit in protest. I look back on my failure to support him as an act of cowardice.

Mostly, however, from 1961 to 1968 I had great satisfaction in teaching, coaching, and learning. During my first year, as I taught one eighth-grade and one twelfth-grade section, I found I related better to older students. In fact, 8th graders drove me crazy. Thus, I asked for and received four twelfth-grade English sections for the next six years. I was the twelfth-grade English teacher, with sections of about eleven to twelve students each. In retrospect, the classroom teaching conditions were unparalleled: I was free to design my own curricula and activities, I had small classes and bright and eager students, and I had a best friend/colleague Nathan "Nat" Reynolds to meet with every day and discuss our craft and our mutual passions for various writers. Once we decided to teach T.S. Eliot's *The Waste Land* simultaneously, he to his tenth-grade classes and I to my twelfth. We had great fun spending an entire weekend going over the poem, line by line, with a few dozen works of criticism spread all over his living room. I'm not sure what the students retained of our well-prepared analysis of Eliot's difficult poem, but I am fairly certain that witnessing two teachers on fire about their subject was itself a valuable experience.

I should note that recently (October 2013), I was invited to the 50th reunion of the class of 1963. In fact, I was the only teacher in attendance. One student presented me with a gift of a new edition of *The Waste Land* (with an introduction by Paul Muldoon). So, apparently, at least one student was affected by it all.

Whether it was Faulkner or Melville (two of Nat's passions) or Frost and Auden (two of mine) or Robert Penn Warren's *All the King's Men* (a mutual favorite), we spent hours every week designing lessons, tests, and essay questions together and arguing or analyzing this or that poem or novel; in the process we forged a lifelong bond. We would arrange our teaching schedules to have the same free period each day to have coffee, talk about teaching, and lament certain aspects of the administration of the school—never dreaming that someday other teachers would be chewing over our limitations as headmasters. Headmaster-bashing being a favorite and time-honored sport among teachers.

Nat and I tried to institute changes within the English department and within the school, but as Nat said, it was like trying to swim in wool. The other faculty members were either terrified of change or enormously irritated by these "young turks," a cliché foisted on us. Our department chair was even distressed about our request to use a variety of paperback novels in our classes; he argued that they weren't "real books." We were almost speechless—but not for long. Every new idea was resisted with "I've been teaching English for twenty years and . . ." Finally, one day Nat, in exasperation, retorted, "No, you haven't. You've taught one year twenty times."

We also tried to launch a school-wide integrated studies plan. The table below is a brief summary of our proposed changes. The faculty listened to our proposal, which we spent months and a hundred or so hours preparing, then overwhelmingly voted it down.

Current Curriculum	Proposed Changes
Stress on rote learning	Emphasis on problem-solving
No arts classes	Strong presence of arts in curriculum
No creative writing instruction	Creative writing added to curriculum
Lectures by teacher	In addition to lectures, student cooperative projects; in-class activities
Tests based on recall of classroom material only	Tests of recall, augmented with analysis and synthesis of material
Athletics consist of competitive sports only	Greater balance in athletics, including fitness and lifetime sports activites

But all the while I was learning what not to do and consequently what I wanted *to do* someday in a school. It was a negative education, but an education nonetheless.

My growing passion for literature and for teaching English led me to approach Father Chalmers with a request: Would he provide a faculty grant for me to attend the Bread Loaf Summer School of English in Vermont during the summer of 1965? He said yes, if I would also visit Eastern colleges and set up a college counseling program for our seniors the following school year. I was excited on both counts.

Bread Loaf (just north of Middlebury, Vermont) was founded in 1920, partly to capitalize on the proximity of Robert Frost, who lived nearby. The classes I took were wonderful, and it was here where I met Elizabeth, my first wife. She was (and is) a black-haired beauty with a brilliant mind, a lovely, shy, graceful manner, and a deep inner life. That summer we took long walks in the Vermont meadows and began meeting after dinner in a courtyard by the dormitories where we would hold each other, kiss, and talk about seeing each other after the summer. In the fall, winter, and spring we saw each other almost every weekend (she was attending graduate school in Claremont), and the idea of marriage rather naturally evolved. We were married in June of 1967.

During this time Nat Reynolds and I volunteered to co-coach junior varsity football. We had both played in high school, and I very briefly in college, and he while in the Army. He coached the defense and I the offense, he the linemen and I the backs. We won some games, lost more, but established even closer relationships with many of our students, who seemed impressed, perhaps even baffled, by two guys who waxed ecstatic about poetry from 8:00 a.m. to 3:00 p.m. and yet, from 3:30 p.m. to 5:30 p.m., seemed knowledgeable about blocking, tackling, running, and passing.

I remember one game in particular, when we had to play a team reputed to be big, mean, and even "dirty." Nat and I decided we needed to toughen up our guys, so we orchestrated a particularly hard week of practice: a lot of heavy scrimmaging, tackling and blocking drills with more than the usual intensity and ferocity, and an uncharacteristic amount of yelling, intimidation, and sarcasm. The kids were shocked but worked hard, and game day arrived. Our kids rose to the occasion, outplayed the other team much of the time, and even led 7–6 with two minutes to go. However, one of our boys fumbled deep in our territory, and the other team scored and won 12–7. Our kids were devastated, but we quickly convinced them that they had "won" what they needed to win. They had conquered their fear of the other team and almost beat them. We thought we had done a great job.

Postscript

About fifteen years later I had one of the members of that team over for dinner. Dave Davis had been in the tenth grade during that JV game and season. He went on to take my twelfth-grade English class, attend Wesleyan University, and become an excellent filmmaker. We stayed in close touch. I liked him immensely. During dinner he told me "that week of practice prior to the 12–7 game" was the worst week of his high school life. He was demoralized by our calling him names ("That was a sissy tackle, Davis") and almost lost all respect for us. He had thought we were sympathetic, sensitive men whom he could trust and admire. That week confused him. I tried to laugh it off over dinner, but his recollections bothered me.

CHAPTER 18

USC and Harvard, 1963–1968:
From PhD to Getting Fired

Love calls us to the things of this world.

—Richard Wilbur

AFTER ABOUT THREE YEARS OF coaching, I had to "retire" because I had begun a graduate program in English at USC. My goal was to earn a PhD and, perhaps, to teach in college someday. I would teach at Harvard in North Hollywood from 8:00 a.m. to 3:00 p.m., and then drive to USC for late-afternoon or evening classes. It was a demanding but exhilarating schedule, despite a series of unexciting first-year classes. One class in traditional grammar, however, taught by William Dean Templeton, a rather schoolmarmy, elderly professor, turned out to be immensely valuable: I was forced to learn grammar, a subject I had hitherto avoided, as we parsed sentences, conjugated verbs, and even diagrammed sentences. I enjoyed it thoroughly.

USC required Ph.D. candidates to take several courses outside the English department, so I took two music-history classes: Music of the Baroque from Alice Ehlers, a delightfully disheveled, disorganized, and eccentric harpsichordist; and Music of the Classic Period from Ingoff Dahl, a superbly organized and brilliant scholar-composer. Both were so invigorating that they inspired me to establish a music-history club for Harvard seniors. A year later, Nat joined forces with me and we persuaded Father Chalmers to allow us to teach a required music and art history class to eighty eighth-graders three times a week. Several students told me years afterward that studying Mozart's Symphony No. 40 or Beethoven's Symphony No. 3 had been a life-changing experience for them.

At USC I found two new passions: poetry and the teaching of one professor, Alan Casson. The two were related, because Casson taught poetry. Week after week, guided by Casson's intelligent insights and close reading, I discovered the brilliance of poems such as "September 1, 1939," "Paysage Moralisé," "Musée des Beaux Arts," and "In Memory of W.B. Yeats." I asked Casson to be my dissertation advisor, and I selected as my topic the poetry of Richard Wilbur, a contemporary poet.

To give myself a crash course in poetry, I began reading books about poetics and metrics. Also, I taught my seniors what I myself was learning. They were my guinea pigs. In retrospect, I was lucky to have chosen books about poetry that I think to this very day are still among the best books available on the subject: Cleanth Brooks's *The Well Wrought Urn*, I.A. Richards's *Practical Criticism*, and John Ciardi's *How Does a Poem Mean?*

Because Wilbur was then in midcareer, having published only four slim volumes, very little had been written about him. I finished my "research" after about three days in the library. The rest of the time I just read and reread the poems. Elizabeth helped me analyze ones I didn't understand, and Nat helped too. Mostly, however, I was guided by Casson, who read my dissertation chapter by chapter and ordered one revision after another. As hard as he forced me to work, I loved doing it, appreciating all the while Wilbur's exquisite craftsmanship. Critics called his poems "cool" (i.e., cerebral), but I found them profoundly moving. One had to go beneath his deceptively simple surfaces to find the passion, but it was there:

> Now swings
> The sky to noon, and mysteries run
> To cover; let our love not blight
> The various world, but trust the flight
> Of love that falls again where it begun,
> All creatures are, and are undone.
> Then lose them, lose
> With love each one,
> And choose
> To welcome love in the lively wasting sun.

Wilbur's poetry was like that of the better-known Wallace Stevens but with a lovelier, less obscure, more human simplicity.

> The garden of the world, which no one sees
> Never had walls, is fugitive with lives;
> Its shapes escape our simpler symmetries;
> There is no resting where it rots and thrives.

The poems reinforced my own growing sense of the need for what Wilbur calls "a difficult balance" in all of life's disparate elements—in society, in the environment, and in each individual's life. In addition, his love poetry is lovely and profound:

> Your hands hold roses always in a way that says
> They are not only yours; the beautiful changes
> In such kind ways,
> Wishing ever to sunder
> Things and things' selves for a second finding, to lose
> For a moment all that it touches back to wonder.

Wilbur also confirmed Frost's notion of this earth as "the right place for love." As critic William Meredith wrote, Wilbur's poetry explores "the human capacity for happiness," asserting "that the universe is decent in the lovely derivative sense of that word." I memorized so many of his poems that I find today, more than forty years later, that lines and stanzas come to mind and often help me make sense of my own universe.

Writing my dissertation was a bracing experience. Alan Casson took his place on my list of lifelong teacher-heroes that began with Daniel Smith and Otis Pease at Stanford. As I tell my colleagues, teachers, and fellow administrators, everyone needs teachers, no matter how old or well-educated we are. When learning is a lifelong adventure, we stay young and alive.

While I studied Richard Wilbur's poems, I made a few futile attempts at writing poems myself. They were horrible—often pale and pathetic reflections of Wilbur—but I discovered the truism that one can learn best by trying to do. It was also about this time, 1966, that I again found myself getting into occasional disagreements with Father Chalmers, the headmaster, after four years of relative calm. I had become a respected member of the faculty, and I had learned how not to antagonize parents while still requiring independent thinking from their sons.

Several incidents from this era still pop into my mind now and then. In fact, one came to mind while I was attending the fiftieth birthday of one of my students from the class of 1964, who had become a lifelong friend. Lee Siegel came to Harvard in his junior year of high school. During his first week at the school, his Spanish teacher asked him whether he knew what a cash register was. "No, sir," Lee replied. "A Jewish piano," his teacher said, laughing. Lee was amazed by the idiocy of the teacher but also horrified to find faculty members expressing such blatant anti-Semitism.

When Lee entered my senior English class, I was pleased to find him a quick, original, imaginative, and exceptionally bright student. Around this time Jack O'Donnell and I had started a literary magazine, *Harvest*, at the school, in which Lee published an anti-war, anti-fascist poem that many students considered unpatriotic. The controversy over the magazine widened.

> Democ(k)razy
> has its
> Fasci-nation:
> when reason
> becomes (t)reason;
> what hATE
> starts to EAT;
> when abom(b) I (nation)
> causes:
> the birds' COO
> the chickens' CLUCKS
> to become the death chant of CLAN
> where mal(ice) exists
> in our (re)public
> or
> in our he(art)s.

The magazine was becoming a hot topic. The editor of the student newspaper wrote an attack on the "obscure and pretentious" writing of Siegel and other *Harvest* contributors. This was better than we could have planned; for a while everyone was reading the magazine and taking sides. *Harvest* was a wonderful experience for us all. It even prompted an encouraging letter I received:

Dear Mr. Cummins:

Presumably my son's final grade has now been determined, and I will not be open to charges of buttering up his instructor if I compliment you on your work with Jonathan. He has been stimulated and awakened by your efforts. This has been reflected in many interesting discussions at home, so we too have been indirectly benefited by your course.

It seems to me that the *Harvest Magazine* is an excellent beginning and a fine thing to have inaugurated at Harvard. I hope that it continues publication and continues to stir up differences of opinion. I like to see these boys stirred up occasionally, even to the point of outrage, pro or con, on any intellectual issue. Also I am sure that the Magazine is going to result in increased awareness at the school of the importance of skill and style in writing.

Please put me down as a supporter of *Harvest* and call on me if I can be of any help next year.

My thanks again for your interest in Jonathan.

Sincerely yours,
Gregory Peck

One other incident stands out in my memory. One day, in my second or third year, I was looking for a student's records. Somehow I found myself in the alumni files. And there they were: my SAT scores. I can honestly say I had no recollection of ever having seen them before. I had been admitted to Stanford in 1955, when SATs were relatively unimportant, and I never paid any attention to standardized tests. When I discovered the scores I was a teacher, a holder of several degrees, twenty-five years old, and feeling fairly self-confident in my chosen field. I was utterly shocked! The scores were amazingly low. I stared at them in disbelief, because now I was a college counselor, and I knew what they meant. Those numbers hit me between the eyes. I was depressed for weeks. Was I really that stupid? How could I be teaching when all my students were more intelligent than I?

Then I began to wonder how much younger students wilt under the weight of scores and grades? How many students wouldn't live up to their potential because a test score or grade gave them a crippling self-image? How many potentially productive students would fail to achieve because they had been made to feel inadequate? By accident or the good fortune of an encouraging teacher, some would be lucky enough to discover that there are many kinds of intelligence.

Over the years I would become convinced that our job as educators is to continually widen our vision of what intelligence is and how we can teach the variety of young people we encounter. Our job as parents is to value the uniqueness of each of our children to give them the self-respect and self-worth that allows for maximum growth. In an earlier chapter I quoted e e cummings's observation that "nothing measurable is worth a good god damn." I am thankful that I never saw my SAT scores when I was seventeen years old. If I had, Crossroads School would probably not exist.

In 1967 my friend Nat Reynolds was offered the position of headmaster of Westlake School, a girls' school in West Los Angeles. He accepted, and I replaced him as chairman of the English department. The department was composed of a few "old guard" members and several of us "young turks," a singularly inappropriate nickname because our "reform" proposals were actually absurdly moderate. Nevertheless, I did enjoy my first administrative position and tried to chair a department with regular meetings, workshops, guest speakers, and presentations to each other on a rotating basis. I was enjoying my first real opportunity to provide some intellectual leadership and design new curricular ideas.

Also in 1967 John White, a former student of mine at Harvard returned to teach (by then I had become the chairman of the English department). One day Father Chalmers called me into his office and told me that John's hair was too long and that I should do something about it. I was caught off guard and mumbled something. I returned in two days and told Father Chalmers that I had thought it over and, first of all, I thought the length of a man's hair should be his own choice, but, in any event, I didn't think that my duties as department chair should include telling teachers how long their hair should be or how they should dress. He scowled and nodded; end of conversation. The next year, John was not invited to return as a teacher, and I helped him find a job at Oakwood, a nearby school. The hair issue with John and the constant discussion in the 1960s of long hair as a repudiation of American values prompted me one night to try again to write a poem. I titled the poem "Advice" and, on a whim, sent it off to *The New Republic* magazine, then forgot about it. Four months later I received a twenty-five dollar check in the mail. I was baffled. I opened a separate envelope and found, to my amazement, a letter from the poetry editor of *The New Republic* telling me they were publishing the poem in the magazine's November 18, 1967, issue. I was exhilarated. It was the first poem I had ever sent to a magazine, and here it was going to be published in a national publication. Elizabeth and I celebrated by going out to dinner with another colleague and his wife.

ADVICE

Oh Father, my Father, Oh what must I do?
They're burning our streets and beating me blue,
"Listen my son, I'll tell you the truth:

Get a close haircut and spit-shine your shoes."

Oh Mother, my Mother, my confusions remove,
I long to embrace her whose hair is so smooth.
"Now listen my son, although you're confused,
Cut your hair close and shine all your shoes."

Oh Teacher, my Teacher, your life with me share,
What books ought I read? What thoughts do I dare?
"Oh Student, my Student, of dissent you beware,
Shine those dull shoes and cut short your hair."

Oh Preacher, my Preacher, does God really care?
Are all races equal? Are laws just and fair?
"Boy—here's the answer, no need to despair:
Shine those new shoes and cut short that hair."

The next day I had the poem in hand as I walked by Father Chalmers's office. His door was open and our eyes met. In my excitement and naïveté I showed him the poem. He read it and without looking up said, "Paul, the English department members are leaving their empty coffee cups in the lounge. Would you take care of it?" He then began shuffling papers—end of encounter.

In retrospect I realize that, in addition to my obvious lack of sensitivity in showing him this particular poem, Father Chalmers probably was disturbed and perhaps even tormented by how much he had to compromise his own beliefs to accommodate the power of his trustees and his conservative parent base. He had once been a radical himself, but Harvard was now in a major capital fundraising campaign and I was probably an annoyance to him.

Nevertheless, in the fall of 1967 Father Chalmers stopped me on campus and told me he thought I was ready to be a headmaster. He said he was sending my name to be placed on a National Association of Independent Schools potential headmaster list. He strolled off. I was shocked. He had never visited one of my classes; he had only reprimanded me in previous years, and I had had little personal contact with him. I was flattered by this newly accorded respect and recognition. I had been thinking of some curriculum reforms that I had hoped to see at Harvard, so I wrote him a long letter in which I made suggestions such as adding arts classes to the curriculum and cutting back on hours spent marching around the drill field. Two weeks after I sent the letter, his secretary arranged for me to see him. I was feeling particularly hopeful about these curriculum ideas—after all, he now saw me as headmaster material, and though he didn't know it, I had recently been his staunch defender during a bizarre meeting in which a trustee had tried, unsuccessfully, to quiz me about Father Chalmers's drinking habits.

I strolled into his headmaster's office only to find one small, bare chair facing his huge, neat desk. He sat on a large leather chair, with a huge cross (the figure of Jesus, bleeding hands and all) on the wall directly behind him. Needless to say, it was a classic "power setup." He gestured for me to sit down. I did. As both he and Jesus looked down on me, he proceeded to lambaste me. Who did I think I was, telling him how to run his school? He became red in the face and continued to harangue me for disrespect and insubordination. "And," he concluded, "you can bloody well teach somewhere else next year!" End of meeting. I hadn't said a word. I got up and left his office and went home. I was numb. I had spent just over one-third of my life at Harvard School. I was thirty years old, and I had gone to Harvard School for four years and taught there for seven. Eleven years, and wham—just like that it was over.

CHAPTER 19

Oakwood School, 1968–1970:
The Moderate as Moderate

The past isn't dead and buried.
In fact, it isn't even past.

—William Faulkner, *Requiem for a Nun*

I FINISHED THE SCHOOL YEAR at Harvard without incident. At graduation, several seniors broke ranks during the procession and came over to the faculty area to shake my hand. It was their gesture of defiance toward Father Chalmers, and I suppose I appreciated their support. I felt wronged and wounded, but by that point I was eager to get away from the place. Also, I was extraordinarily depressed by what had happened on June 4, 1968.

That evening I was watching television as Elizabeth was correcting papers in the other room. I was rejoicing in Robert Kennedy's triumph in the California primary election that day and was fantasizing about his being elected president in November. I had seen him at the Greek Theatre about six weeks earlier delivering what remains etched in my memory as the single most dramatic, inspiring political speech I have ever heard. Bobby was on fire: his key themes were the civil-rights movement and how to end the Vietnam calamity. But what was most electrifying was his passion.

As the tragedy of his assassination unfolded on TV, I started sobbing; it was as though I had lost a personal friend. Elizabeth heard me weeping and came running into the room. It was an utterly devastating blow that made those of all political persuasions wonder whether the country had gone berserk. Just five years after the assassination of President John F. Kennedy, there had been two more in the space of a few months: Martin Luther King, Jr. and now Robert Kennedy. The forces of bigotry and hate seemed to have been unleashed upon the land. Biblical prophecies about the end times and "the reaping of whirlwinds" seemed all too terrifyingly apt.

Within two weeks of being fired, I had received a call from Hamlin Smith, the headmaster of neighboring Oakwood School. He was looking for an assistant headmaster. I was pleased by his interest, and we met. I explained to him that I had already signed a contract with UCLA to be a part-time teaching assistant in the English department, but he said he would be willing to have me come to Oakwood three days a week. Between the two part-time jobs I could earn a full-time salary of about $12,000 a year. So in September of 1968 I became assistant headmaster of Oakwood School on Monday, Wednesday, and Friday and a teaching assistant in UCLA's freshman composition program on Tuesday and Thursday. It was the beginning of many years in which I would serve two institutions simultaneously.

Oakwood School was definitely a novel experience for me, like walking from a desert into a rain forest. Unlike Harvard, Oakwood was a coeducational, progressive, New Age kind of place. Unlike the somber and stern Father Chalmers, Hamlin Smith was a big, affectionate bear of a man. He loved young people, and they loved him. The whole place exuded warmth, friendliness, and affection. At Harvard I had been the resident radical; here I was initially perceived as a conservative. For the first month, I insisted that my students call me "Mr. Cummins," even though they called all their other teachers by their first names. I was also annoyed when I came into a room to teach and found the chairs not arranged in an orderly manner. "Relax, man," a senior said to me.

"It's not 'man,'" I replied. "It's Mr. Cummins." He rolled his eyes and shook his head in mock dismay. In time I adjusted, and so did the students. It is said that the flip side of any virtue is a related vice. Harvard had been relatively uncreative but orderly; Oakwood was creative but a bit sloppy. I was probably a moderate, with many at Harvard to my right and many at Oakwood to my left.

Having girls in class added a whole new sensibility to the dynamics of the classroom. I resolved never again to teach in a single-sex school. One year at Culver and seven at Harvard had been enough. I clearly understand the arguments in favor of single-sex education, especially for girls, who are often overshadowed as teachers give boys permission to dominate. But as a teacher I found that girls added a sensitive understanding of relationships in literature and life that often escaped the typically insecure adolescent boy. There was far less posing by girls and far less need to show off one's intelligence and insights.

The Oakwood boys were also different from Harvard students. Macho attitudes were frowned upon, and the arts were valued. Many Oakwood boys were excellent musicians; some were first-rate writers and artists, right alongside the girls. Often students would not only write an excellent essay on a given work of literature but would add to it a drawing or painting, completely on their own initiative. For example, after receiving an essay assignment that had to do with a frog, one girl gave me a wonderfully whimsical, huge papier-mâché frog painted in wild greens, blues, and oranges. I still treasure it.

Because creativity was so obviously encouraged at Oakwood, I came to learn that the arts truly enliven a curriculum. Ham Smith and his staff were all over the campus praising kids for their work, laughing, and empathizing with them. Ham created an environment unlike anything I had ever seen in a school before and was also a major influence on my later approaches to school administration.

Every Wednesday evening, I met with Ham, his wife Shirley Smith, and a trustee named Jack Zimmerman, who also taught part-time math, for an informal dinner and an administrative roundtable meeting that often lasted several hours. The administrative model was the circle. There was no person at the top making decisions as there had been at Harvard School. We talked over an issue until we reached a consensus. Sometimes there were wild disagreements, but we always ultimately found a resolution. It is a style of administration that I found to be as "right as rain" and one that I have tried to implement ever since. Certainly Crossroads School and New Roads School were the beneficiaries of those long-ago Wednesday-evening meetings.

At Oakwood in those days there were several other "new" approaches to education. As I mentioned earlier, students called their teachers by their first names. To students, this sent an important message: the teacher is not just your mentor-instructor-challenger, but also your friend, supporter, and confidant, should you need one. This simple practice sets a radically different tone at the school. Also, at Oakwood, administrators' doors were always open, and students felt free to wander in and discuss problems, seek help, or just talk. At first I was annoyed, complaining loudly, "I can't get my work done."

Shirley Smith, my office mate, just smiled and replied, "This *is* our work."

Oakwood was not a politically wild campus; it was a place open to viewing American politics and institutions with a critical eye. During this time, I had read two books by Richard Hofstadter that had a striking impact on my own thinking: *Anti-Intellectualism in American Life* and *The Paranoid Style in American Politics*. Both heightened my growing apprehension about the right wing's quest for simple "answers" to complex social and political issues. I was also disturbed by the expanding brand of "super-patriotism" that had led from the Red-baiting of Senator Joe McCarthy, the treatment of J. Robert Oppenheimer, the popularity of George Wallace and Curtis LeMay, and the rise of Richard Nixon, to the John Birch Society, the Ku Klux Klan, and the National Rifle Association.

At Oakwood, I taught two senior English classes, and at UCLA, I taught two or three sections of freshman composition. Elizabeth was also an English teacher, at Cal State Northridge, so our evenings were invariably consumed with correcting essays and lesson planning. The combination of teaching and administrative duties was grueling, even though I liked all of it. Finally, I decided that I could only handle one job. In the fall of 1969 Ham Smith offered me a full-time administrative position for the following year, and I agreed to take it. However, other events transpired that caused me to reconsider.

Although I was unaware of it, Oakwood's Board of Trustees was becoming more and more concerned about Ham Smith's "loose administrative style," and they finally determined to replace him. Over the 1969 Christmas break his close friend, Jack Zimmerman, also a trustee, had to inform Ham that he, Jack, would be replacing him next year as headmaster. It was a bitter blow for Ham, a terribly painful experience for Jack, and a source of confusion and disappointment for me.

Although Jack asked me to stay on as his assistant headmaster, at that time I had also been approached by Abbott Academy, a girls' school in Andover, Massachusetts, which was looking for an assistant headmaster. Soon after this call from Abbott (and a subsequent visit to its campus), I received a call from Nat Reynolds, who was on the Board of Trustees of St. Augustine's-by-the-Sea Episcopal Elementary School, which was seeking a headmaster. I was paralyzed with indecision. Jack had become a good friend, although I could not have imagined the role he would play in my life in future years. Don Gordon, the head at Abbott, was also an impressive man. However, I was, to tell the truth, intrigued by the idea of becoming a headmaster myself. I stalled. Finally, the chair of St. Augustine's selection committee told me he would be calling me at noon on a Friday in mid-May. At 11:30 a.m. I took a walk and returned home, still undecided. When the phone rang at noon, I heard my voice telling him, yes, I would take the position.

Father Figures

And you, my father, there on the sad height,
Curse, bless me now with your fierce tears, I pray,
Do not go gentle into that good night.
Rage, rage against the dying of the light.

—Dylan Thomas,
"Do Not Go Gentle into That Good Night"

EARLIER CHAPTERS HAVE TOUCHED ON my father's pervasive influence on me. Though in adopting a liberal stance in politics I rejected his politically conservative outlook, the fact remains that his fundamental values are the bedrock of my character. Throughout my career, I visited my dad often. I dropped by at any time of day or night, unannounced, whenever I felt lonely or needed to talk. We would shoot baskets, play pool, or just sit and talk. He was my friend, and I adored him. His stories, his sense of humor, his gentle patience, and his unconditional love had been the strong foundation for my sister and me all our lives.

Although he had been a wonderful athlete and had always urged me to take care of my body, Dad hadn't practiced what he preached. He ate junk food and drank too much. Gradually his arteries clogged and his kidneys began to fail. In 1982 he went on dialysis. When he developed kidney failure, I tried not to think about ultimate consequences. But one day, we both had a moment of foreboding. As we sat in his living room, he said, "Come outside; I'll beat you at a game of 21." I bantered back at him, and we went outside. He took a couple of short shots at the basket but lacked the strength even to get the ball up to the rim.

I said, "Oh, forget it; I'm not in the mood, anyway." But we both knew that his end was near.

with
my dad

His kidneys got worse, and he lost more weight. In 1983, when the doctor said he must increase the dialysis sessions to three times a week, he said, "No." The doctor told us that we must persuade him to comply or else he would die. I begged him to do it, but he said, "Son, it's time to go. I've lived a good life, but the quality of my physical life is now so poor . . . it's time to call it a day." He quit going to dialysis altogether, knowing that he would be comatose in three to five days. We spent the next four days saying our goodbyes. On Saturday afternoon, March 23, I knew that the final curtain was about to close. I held him and told him again how much I loved him. By 7:00 p.m. he had virtually lost consciousness, and we called the paramedics, because his wife, Sue, didn't want him to die at home. We drove with him to the hospital; he was now fully comatose. I found myself hoping that maybe he would wake up in the hospital, and we could resume our loving relationship. Life without him was simply inconceivable to me. From about 8:00 p.m. to 5:00 a.m. the next morning, I walked up and down the hall of the hospital, looking in on him every ten minutes or so. He was breathing in short, raspy breaths. When I looked in at about 5:00 a.m., the nurse was there by the bedside. She nodded at me. I froze and then heard a wail come forth from somewhere deep inside me. It was a sound of deep anguish, and it startled me. Then I walked over to him and kissed his face, told him I loved him, and left the room. It was over.

For the service we held several days later, I wrote a piece that I asked a friend to read. It concluded with the following:

> I don't know if the wellsprings of my tears will ever dry up. My father was the best father a boy and a man could ever have, the best friend a son could hope for. In the great mystery of death and the great beyond, in the days of my own life to come, I will love the man from the depths of my soul. That is his legacy to me, and that is my tribute to him.

I lost my father in 1983. It might not even be coincidental that about that time I became friends with Dr. Herbert Zipper. I had met Herbert Zipper briefly in 1974, shortly after Mary Ann had heard him speak at a conference and came home raving about this seventy-year-old ardent advocate of the arts.

During the early 1980s, when I was endeavoring to expand the arts at Crossroads, I asked Herbert Zipper to serve on our board to help me "sell" the arts to our more apprehensive board members. (It seems as though one is always having to "sell" the arts in America.) He joined and was quite persuasive as we instituted our "arts-majors" programs. In fact, he and I in a sense "signed up" USC as a partner in our new program. (Later, a USC administrator would reprimand him for overstepping his bounds, but the interlocking of institutional logos was helpful for several years.)

In 1985, partially because of Crossroads's success and in part because I was exhausted from the fifteen-year challenge of launching and building the school, I approached my Board of Trustees and asked for a five-month sabbatical. I wanted to engage myself in a project far afield from Crossroads. I wanted to read and write but not necessarily about education per se.

It seemed as though each time I had encountered Herbert Zipper, I had heard another vignette about his life that piqued my curiosity. Before my sabbatical began, I approached him to ask whether I might write a brief biography of him. I had in mind a twenty- to thirty-page pamphlet to record and thereby preserve some key events of his life; at that time I had no idea of the extent of his adventures, ordeals, and achievements. He agreed, and after Mary Ann and I spent the first month (July of 1985) of my sabbatical traveling in England and Scotland, I returned to what I thought was my four-month project of writing a short pamphlet.

In August I went to Herbert's home for the first interview, taking along a notepad and a tape recorder. The first few interviews were a revelation to me. His life was rich and dense beyond my wildest expectations. A four-month activity became a major five-year project. I managed to complete a skeleton first draft of about 220 pages before returning to my headmaster duties, but there was all sorts of research to do in areas that had impinged upon Herbert's life including the Hapsburg Em-

pire, fin-de-siècle Vienna, Austria and World War I, the events leading to the Anschluss, the Holocaust, and the Philippines during World War II, and so on. I
set out to read everything I could find on these subjects, thinking that someday
Crossroads might establish a room in the school library dedicated to Zipper's life.
Whatever reading and writing time I could find came late at night, on weekends, or
in the early mornings. Even more difficult than finding time to write was finding
a way to get "inside" Herbert. He was such an extraordinarily project- and work-
driven man that his own interior life was either closed off or so subordinated to
achievement that he waved away the normal fears and demons most people face.
Try as I might, I could only get him to talk about the external events of his life. At
first, I felt almost like a stenographer, recording his autobiography. Gradually, I
became aware of some of his foibles and limitations, but my book would not read
like contemporary Freudian biographies. It is not a deep character analysis; rather
it is the story of one man's encounter with a terrible century, of the capacity of the
human will to triumph under conditions of unspeakable brutality. Herbert Zipper
was not a well-known figure, but he was a remarkable global patriot, whose life and
vision will outlast him and reverberate through many lives.

with Bruno Bettelheim, Herbert Zipper, and
Warren Spaeth

I would come home from my daily interviews and excitedly tell Mary Ann what
I had learned. Herbert's stories became part of our family lore, and the characters in his life became twentieth-century heroes to us all. My daughters read early
drafts of the book and by doing so further absorbed his values and work ethic.
Knowing him made us all less trivial.

Finally, by 1991 I had put together a 300-page biography and had secured a
publisher, the Peter Lang Publishing Company. The first edition of 2,000 copies
sold out, a second edition of another 2,000 sold out, and the book is now in a fourth

printing. Perhaps more importantly, the book has received wonderful reviews and delighted hundreds of Zipper's friends and acquaintances. There have been some unexpected additional benefits as well. First, the book was translated into Chinese in 1993 (an edition that sold more than 4,000 copies) with a second edition in 1997; later it was also translated into a German-Austrian edition that has sold more than 3,000 copies to date. The book was also the basis for a documentary film made by Terry Sanders and Freida Lee Mock of the American Film Foundation; the film, *Never Give Up: The 20ᵗʰ Century Odyssey of Herbert Zipper*, was nominated for an Academy Award in 1996. Ultimately, my idea for a twenty- to thirty-page pamphlet took on a life of its own. As I look back, I consider the book, *Dachau Song: The Twentieth-Century Odyssey of Herbert Zipper*, published in 1992, to be one of the more important achievements of my life.

While a brief summary of Herbert's life is impossible, the following is a bare outline:

Herbert Zipper was born in 1904 in Vienna in the Hapsburg Empire. As a boy he watched Emperor Franz Joseph's carriage pass by his house. He was educated in the finest academies, studying under Richard Strauss and Maurice Ravel, among others, and became a conductor-composer in Germany in the early 1930s. When Hitler became chancellor, he hastened back to Vienna, where he composed music for the underground cabarets of his day. In 1938, after the Anschluss, he was sent to Dachau and transferred to Buchenwald (1939).

His survival stories are remarkable. These stories include the formation at Dachau of a secret orchestra for which he composed music, conducted, and gave clandestine concerts in an abandoned latrine. He and a prison-mate, Jura Soyfer, also composed a song, "The Dachau Lied," which was to have an extraordinary history. He was released from Buchenwald and journeyed to Manila to marry the love of his life and to conduct the Manila Symphony Orchestra. When the Japanese invaded, he was put in prison again. After five months of interrogation, he was released, worked for the underground, and a few weeks after the liberation of Manila, organized out of the rubble of the city an extraordinary concert.

After the war he came to America and founded more than a dozen community arts schools and was an internationally effective educator. In his eighties and nineties he visited China ten times, teaching conductors, composers, and instrumentalists about Western music. Thus, his life spanned virtually three centuries: from the nineteenth-century Hapsburg Empire through the horrors of World War II and the rise of China as a major economic power.

Throughout his remarkable journey, Zipper, a composer, conductor, concentration camp survivor, and educator, maintained a spirit of hope and achievement that contradicts his experiences. His is a story of the triumph of human will and spirit.

Herbert became a major inspiration to me. His life illustrated the impact a single individual can have upon a larger community. Knowing Herbert, I came to value time even more and to be ever less patient with its trivial expenditures. Through Herbert's eyes, I came to see even more clearly the unique importance of the arts in the lives of each individual and each nation. Finally, his commitment to public education inspired me to go beyond Crossroads to reach out into a wider arena. At first, this wider arena consisted of expanding the work of the Crossroads Community Foundation. Next, I would create a new entity—the New Visions Foundation, whose mission would be to start new schools that would serve low-income, highly at-risk students.

In 1997 this major chapter in my life came to a wrenching close. Herbert informed me in November of 1996 that he had been diagnosed with lung cancer and that his doctor had recommended immediate chemotherapy. Mary Ann and I were extremely upset. We knew that at ninety-two, Herbert would not be around much longer, but he had become a fixture in our lives. It was hard to imagine his absence. I had visited him every Sunday for ten years, almost without fail, at 8:00 a.m. sharp. We would discuss everything from education to politics to whatever subject took our fancy. He would have dinner with us every Monday evening at precisely 7:30. Also, he taught counterpoint (a complex part of music theory) with Mary Ann at Crossroads.

By January, a miracle had occurred. The cancer was gone—not a trace. However, he was getting weaker and weaker. The chemotherapy had killed the cancer, but it probably also hastened his overall decline. In mid April, he entered Santa Monica Hospital. Consequently, the following Sunday, April 20th, I assumed he would not expect me at our usual 8:00 a.m. time. At 8:10 a.m. I received a call from his niece, Lucy, who asked, "Where are you?" At 7:59 a.m., Herbert had awakened, sat upright, and at 8:00 a.m. on the dot, asked, "Where's Paul?" I told Lucy I planned to be there at 4:00 p.m. Herbert slept most of the day, but at 3:59 p.m. woke up and at 4:00 p.m. sharp and asked Lucy, "Where's Paul?" I arrived at 4:02 p.m., and he was slightly miffed at my lack of punctuality.

During our visit, I noticed that he was having trouble focusing on conversation. I brought up a problem I was having at the new school. Suddenly, he became alert and cogent. Education remained his passion even during his last conscious moments. The next morning, April 21st, 1997, I was giving a faculty workshop at a downtown public school when I received a call with the message "Come quickly."

By the time I arrived, he was gone, his mouth frozen agape. A few weeks later I wrote the following poem:

THE DEATH OF A FRIEND

When the call finally came
I was doing his kind of work—
encouraging teachers to value the arts.
"He's dying," they told me. I rushed to my car.
When I arrived his face was frozen
mouth agape in a death masque
the body rigid as the Goethe monument
we both admired years ago.
I stepped out in the hall a moment
to let the tears flow uncontrolled
before returning to the others.
At ninety-two he had come to seem
as one who might escape mortality.
His memory never retreated from reality,
his mind never left the room.
The lights were simply shut off on him.
What he left behind is as hard to measure
as ancient melodies or the surprises of the sea—
you know they are there but just precisely where
is a matter of surmise.
I only know that I knew him well
and I will never be the same.

After Herbert's death, *Dachau Song* went into a third and, in 2014, a fourth edition. What follows comes from a preface to the third edition, which I wrote in 2001:

Herbert is gone now, and my wife and family and I miss him dearly. Nevertheless, his legacy remains and continues to inspire people across the globe. His presence in many people's lives is also evidenced by a series of factors. For one, the concert hall at the Colburn School, named after his friend Richard Colburn, is itself named Zipper Hall. In addition, at my school, Crossroads School, our library has a special collections room—The Herbert Zipper Room—which contains his music and books, letters, photographs, memorabilia, and a large collection of books about the Hapsburg Empire, Vienna in the 19th and 20th centuries, the Holocaust (particularly his books about Dachau and Buchenwald), and other events relating to his life and times. Thirdly, there is a new and expanded version of his Dachau Lied, orchestrated by composer Lucas Richman, which has had several performances in the United States and is available through the Herbert Zipper library at Crossroads School.

Finally, there is a wonderful video of his life, *Never Give Up*, which was created by Terry Sanders and Frieda Lee Mock, friends of Herbert's and Academy Award winners. *Never Give Up* (available through Crossroads) was itself nominated for an Academy Award and has been shown in theaters and on television all across the country.

New Roads and New Visions

1990 Onward

We have heard the chimes at midnight.

—Shakespeare

CHAPTER 20

From the Yellow Pages to P.S. Arts and the Greater Community

. . . Because everything can happen
on the other side of the door.

—Jeff Moss

MY "SECOND EDUCATION" BEGAN WITH reading the Yellow Pages. I was sitting at my desk one day in 1990, feeling particularly pleased with Crossroads—its achievements, reputation, and overall "solidness." But I was also feeling increasingly unsettled by a feeling of being uninformed about public education in Los Angeles and most of all, unaware of what conditions were like in my own backyard. On a whim, I decided to visit some local public schools. I got out the Yellow Pages and called the principals of about seven schools, introduced myself, and invited myself over for a visit. At first they were puzzled, perhaps even suspicious. Why did the headmaster of a private school want to visit their schools?

Up to this time, my knowledge of day-to-day operations in public schools was limited to what I heard on the news or read in magazine and newspaper articles. I had vague impressions of inept principals, lazy and uninvolved teachers, bureaucratic waste, overcrowded classrooms, and ugly campuses. I was right about the latter two points—but not much else. I was surprised to meet many bright, competent, and creative principals, and a host of first-rate teachers operating on budgets that had been cut down to the bare minimum.

I found shocking conditions—even in the relatively wealthy sections of Los Angeles. I found schools with virtually no PE teachers, no arts teachers, no reading or math specialists, no librarians, and no counselors. I found schools with huge turnovers of transient students—the progeny of unemployed, unfortunate, homeless, immigrant, non-English-speaking parents. In one particular school, the third-grade teacher had begun a school year in September with thirty students, and by March she had thirty different students: a 100 percent turnover! "My God," I said to the principal, "how can you teach under such conditions?"

"You tell me," she responded.

I was surprised to visit an elementary school with 740 students, one principal, and one secretary. "At my high school [grades six through twelve]," I told the principal, "we also have 740 students, but we have a headmaster, assistant headmaster, director of middle school, director of upper school, four deans, and seven secretaries." He simply shook his head in tired resignation. I found schools with minimal maintenance crews and no security guards. Some schools refused to receive gifts such as computers or film projectors, because the schools would be broken into and vandalized, and, of course, the gifts would be stolen. The biggest surprise was how much of this existed in my own backyard.

Every day the children in these schools brought to class emotional, social, and cultural realities that teachers had to try to accommodate. Often many languages were spoken in one classroom. Then there were the profound emotional issues: children who were neglected, abused and hungry; children who lacked proper medical and dental care; children had who come from families with no books; children who were afraid to play in neighborhood parks because of gangs; children with family members who had been shot at or murdered; children who didn't know who their fathers were; and children who were exposed to "adult activities" they never should have seen. These young children truly were victims of their environment. They had done nothing wrong except to have had the misfortune of being born into poverty. These teachers were fighting an uphill battle upon terrain growing steeper and uglier by the year. My "antique liberalism" was receiving daily reaffirmation.

As I drove across town visiting public schools, I saw neighborhoods that were for all intents and purposes entirely segregated. One parochial school I visited was 96 percent African American, another public school was about 90 percent Hispanic and 99 percent non-Caucasian. Here we are, I thought, forty years after the historic 1954 *Brown v. Board of Education* decision, and many of our schools are less integrated than before 1954.

As I walked through these schools, I couldn't help but look at the children and wonder what sort of future awaited them. Many would undoubtedly drop out by the end of ninth grade and enter the street culture of gangs, drugs, crime, and, ultimately, the prison system. I looked at their incredibly beautiful and innocent faces and became alternately sad and angry. I was reminded of Jonathan Kozol's words in his book *Savage Inequalities*: "Surely there is enough for everyone within this country . . . All our children ought to be allowed a stake in the enormous richness of America . . . They are all quite wonderful and innocent when they are small. We soil them needlessly."

I began to fear that these children would have little stake in the country. America was now divided into five classes: an elite group of the super-rich, a second tier of the rich, a middle class, a lower class, and an anonymous underclass. The first two are wallowing in wealth, while the bottom three are dying. How can we allow this? What, I began to wonder, had happened to our basic sense of fairness?

Launching P.S. Arts

All of this was not only depressing, it was also eye-opening. I had read about such conditions in Kozol's *Death at an Early Age* back in 1967, but seeing these realities with my own eyes was far more startling. At nearby Palms Middle School I casually asked the vice principal, Lana Brody, whether there was anything my school could do to help. She replied that since Crossroads had such wonderful arts programs, perhaps we could help in this area. "That's easy," I said, "we'll 'loan' you our choral teacher a couple of hours a week." So we sent our terrific choral director, Thea Kano, to Palms to start an after-school program, with Crossroads paying for her time. About eighty kids showed up, and Thea first built an after-school chorus, then another during school hours. The Palms children, faculty, administration, and parents were all delighted. I secured a small grant from American Express to cover Thea's salary, and this was how my "second education" began to unfold.

The Palms grant suggested a new way of thinking. Why, I asked myself, have we divided education so rigidly between private and public? Why shouldn't the two sectors support each other and share resources? If we could help one public school with our curricular and fundraising resources, then why not others? Why couldn't private schools participate as well? At that time, I had a chance meeting with a Crossroads parent who would have a profound impact on my life. I met musician Herb Alpert at a ninth-grade Crossroads potluck dinner. We began talking about the state of the arts in Los Angeles. I mentioned my recent visits to various public schools and how the arts were either anemic or had been eliminated altogether. He was appalled and told me he had a foundation that would be able to help. We talked, met, and designed a plan to infuse one school with a comprehensive arts program.

The Herb Alpert Foundation pledged a three-year grant of $300,000 to fund music, visual arts, dance, and drama at one public elementary school. Herb and I selected Broadway Elementary School—a low-income, 90 percent Hispanic school in Venice, not far from Crossroads. Broadway's morale was as low as could be, and several teachers were planning to quit or take early retirement. Without overstating the case, the infusion of arts into the school marked a turnaround. Every child received instruction in music, art, dance, and drama—every week, all year, at all grade levels. The halls came alive with children's art, with murals, with the sounds of music and dance. One teacher withdrew her resignation; another canceled her early-retirement plans. The children, starved for opportunities for self-expression, were fed the arts and responded with enthusiasm.

After launching the Herb Alpert program at Broadway in 1993, I set out to do the same at Coeur d'Alene Elementary, which was an equally poor school but more racially mixed. It also had the additional problem of being identified as a school for homeless and immigrant children. It too had virtually no programs in the arts. We received foundation support for Coeur d'Alene from visionary foundations such as the Dougherty Foundation, the Barbra Streisand Foundation, the Heller Financial Group, the Roth Family Foundation, the Plum Foundation, and the Los Angeles Department of Cultural Affairs and launched a comprehensive program at Coeur d'Alene in September of 1994. Teachers were inspired, parents were thrilled, and children were delighted. The growth of school pride was reflected in 1995 when the school received a Redbook Award as one of the 140 finest elementary schools in the country. Principal Beth Ojena credits the arts program with being a major factor in that award.

With two comprehensive arts programs and a choral program in place, I was utterly pleased by this new adventure that was unfolding. However, one night I awoke with a start and a panicky thought: *My God, how are we going to keep the programs functioning from year to year?* I had been so excited by the initial grants we had received that I hadn't looked further down the road. I didn't want to be just another liberal do-gooder whose initial gift evaporated, leaving children even more discouraged than before, having had a taste of something better before being plunged back into deprivation. My co-partner in launching these programs was Alva Libuser, the director of foundation development at Crossroads. We talked over this dilemma and concluded that we needed to create our own foundation to secure ongoing funding. Ultimately, we brought the plan to a Board of Trustees meeting. The concept was unanimously approved—we would launch into a whole new arena.

So with the blessings of the Board of Trustees, we created a separate nonprofit foundation, the Crossroads Community Foundation (CCF), which had as its initial mission the funding of Broadway, Coeur d'Alene, and a new project: setting up after-school programs in music, art, dance, and drama at the Boys & Girls Clubs of Santa Monica.

We wanted to create programs that would build skills, discover and develop talent, and encourage students to see the arts as a solid sequential subject, a potential college focus, perhaps even a career. Certainly, I wanted the arts to become an inducement for students to come to school and not drop out. Brief exposure would not achieve these goals. Our mantra at CCF, which later morphed into P.S. Arts, has been that the arts must be "skill-building and sequential," i.e., what students learned in one grade would be built upon in the next. We took the same approach to faculty I had used at Crossroads: hire first-rate artists who also know how to teach. Practicing artists bring their classes to a deeper understanding of the essence of the arts. They teach and help their students express their artistic goals from the inside out. The trick was to help each individual student find his or her own voice.

One day at Broadway, the principal was walking down the hall when the third-grade teacher stopped him, saying, "You should see José's painting; he just finished it after six weeks of work."

"What are you talking about?" the principal exclaimed. "José was expelled four weeks ago!" He was, it turns out, a "drop-in"; he wanted to finish his art piece—it was that important to him.

The successes at Broadway and Coeur d'Alene were stunning. They helped build enrollment, gained awards for the school, increased attendance, enlivened faculty members, and genuinely improved campus morale. After two years of these successes, the two music teachers, Marty Fox and Richard Gere, came to me with a dilemma. "Our kids are really getting good," they said.

"So what is the problem?" I asked.

"They go on to Mark Twain Middle School, where there is no music program." I could see it coming. Couldn't the CCF expand by at least adding music at Mark Twain, which most of our kids attended next? At the CCF board meeting, we decided to increase our funding goals and add Mark Twain.

Then, in the fall of 1994, I received a phone call from Kip Cohen, the executive director of the Herb Alpert Foundation. Herb was upset, he told me, with the government cuts to the National Endowment for the Arts budget and the general undervaluing of the arts in this country. Could we add a couple more schools to our program if he provided the funds? And could we do this immediately? The CCF board and I were thrilled. We determined to add visual arts programs to two low-income and racially mixed schools—Playa del Rey Elementary and Grand View Boulevard Elementary—in the spring, then add music programs at each of these in the fall. So we began the 1995–96 school year with five schools covered by our funding: four elementary schools and one middle school. We began the 1996–97 school year with an operating budget of $430,000, under which about 2,000 children received weekly instruction in the arts. By 2013-14 the operating budget was $3.1 million, and more than 15,000 children were receiving weekly arts instruction.

Around this time, *Education Week* ran an article praising the school's outreach program. The article began:

> Some people might call Paul Cummins crazy. Like many a private school official, Mr. Cummins, the president of the Crossroads School for Arts and Sciences here, has devoted untold hours to fundraising. And he is good at it. His efforts on a recent campaign paid off to the tune of nearly $1 million. But then he labored just as furiously to give it all away—and to the public schools. It was time for a new challenge, and Mr. Cummins and his colleagues decided they wanted to try to help local cash-strapped public schools restore their largely extinct arts programs.

It then offered several testimonials:

> While partnerships between private and public schools are becoming increasingly common across the nation, the scope of the Crossroads initiative is "pretty impressive," said Margaret Goldsborough, a spokeswoman for the National Association of Independent Schools. "It really has been an overwhelming success story," said Kip Cohen, the President of the Herb Alpert Foundation. He praised the Crossroads program's depth and continuity, contrasting it with programs "where they haul [the students] off to a symphony concert underfed and underslept and underprepared . . . and they call that exposure to the arts."
>
> Among foundations that have been impressed by Crossroads is the ARCO Foundation, the philanthropic arm of the Los Angeles based petroleum company. The foundation "went way out of our guidelines" to approve a $10,000 grant, according to its president, Eugene Wilson. "Typically, we wouldn't give to a private school," he said, "but because they're using an innovative approach with a public school, and in a public school, and with a bunch of at-risk kids, that was enough for us to help them out."

Herb Alpert was the major inspirational player in all this growth, providing more than $743,000 for the arts during the first seven years of the program. His commitment to the arts and to children has inspired us all. He has provided a model for other foundations and individuals. In addition, I thoroughly enjoyed getting to know Herb and his immensely talented wife, Lani—a superb singer. Herb's easy manner, generosity, and humor were a joy to behold and experience. I particularly remember a graduation speech he gave to the New Roads seniors. In urging them to "pursue their passions," he commented on how "I still wake up every morning looking forward to seeing what I can do with those three valves [of a trumpet]."

During the first nine years of P.S. Arts, I functioned as executive director, with two program directors serving as day-to-day administrators. In 2005 I handed the reins to a full-time executive director and thereafter served primarily as a board member, helping mostly with fundraising. By 2010 my title and role would once again evolve to founder/trustee emeritus, allowing me to focus more on new projects.

P.S. Arts has become a leading nonprofit organization in the arts. Its growth was helped enormously in 1997 when Laurie David became president of the board and enlisted several new trustees to help launch the organization's first fundraising event, Express Yourself: A Wonderful Day of Family, Food, and Arts for Children. This event grew to net between $700,000 and $1 million per year.

The organization's insistence upon providing children with programs that are within the school day and are sequential and skill-building sets it apart from other programs. No one would suggest that math should be offered as an "exposure" program, or literature and math as after-school programs. Why treat the arts any differently?

CHAPTER 21

New Visions Foundation/New Roads School

You need to love the thing you do.

—Thomas Lux, "An Horation Notion"

MY EXPOSURE TO THE SEGREGATION in public schools left me wanting to do something about the problem. I came to see that America remains a profoundly segregated society and that all Americans suffer from the effects of this reality. I decided to create a school that had true diversity as its core mission. The concept for what eventually became New Roads School began to take shape.

My first, albeit naïve, effort along these lines was the result of a really dumb idea, which began on one of my site visits to check up on our outreach arts programs at a local public school. On this particular day in the spring of 1993, I was walking across the immense crumbling, wavy asphalt yard at Coeur d'Alene Elementary, looking at ugly buildings, and feeling particularly sad that poor children are not only subjected to blighted neighborhoods and institutionalized poverty, but can't even attend decent-looking schools. I had what I thought was a breakthrough idea. "Yes!" I said out loud in excitement.

Why not create a new entity? A hybrid school: a public school/private school joint venture? Here was this huge, underutilized campus with space to build more buildings, to lay in grass playing fields for soccer and other sports—all of which the surrounding neighborhood could use as well. I began to envision the place as a center of progressive education and community service—an entirely new educational model. We could draw students from Crossroads School's huge waiting list and double the size of Coeur d'Alene with tuition-paying students. Coeur d'Alene had 200 students with per-pupil funding of about $4,000. My idea was to add 200 students paying $10,000 each, thus creating an average expenditure of about $7,000 per pupil. In effect, each tuition-paying family would be subsidizing less fortunate students by $3,000, and we would thereby create a unique community of rich and poor, Caucasian, African American, Hispanic, and Asian. This community would reflect the true diversity of the city as a whole.

It was such an intoxicating prospect that I never really examined the key premise: that I could persuade 200 people to pay $10,000 (Crossroads tuition at the time) to send their children "down to" an ugly public school campus in a poorer part of town (even though I planned to remodel it). I never got to test that premise, however, because there were other more immediate roadblocks. The first obstacle was the faculty at Coeur d'Alene. Principal Beth Ojena and I had decided to structure this plan as a conversion to a charter school, which meant that 70 percent of the faculty would have to vote "yes" on the change. After many meetings, we managed to convince enough of them to give it a go. Then we had to deal with the Los Angeles Unified School District (LAUSD). Several officials wondered whether it was even constitutional to have tuition-paying children attend a public school. We decided we would have to seek special state legislation to allow the experiment. I made a presentation before the LAUSD Board of Education and, surprisingly, received a positive response. I was encouraged. Then a sort of bomb dropped: the teachers' union entered the scene.

In short, Helen Bernstein, then president of United Teachers Los Angeles, declared war on the idea. She, her vice president, and her lawyer all appeared, uninvited, at one of our weekly meetings in December of 1993 and put the fear of God into the faculty. If this idea went through, Bernstein warned, they were risking their pensions as well as future job placements. Later, I went down to Bernstein's office to ask her why she was so hostile to an idea that would benefit children. I received a blast of attitude, a threat to unionize my own private school, and the vow that tuition and/or nonunion teachers would never become part of a public school campus. I left the meeting baffled and angry. I had always believed unions to be a part of the progressive tradition in America, and here was one blocking a simple, small, experimental idea. Los Angeles public schools were then, as now, in crisis, and any new thinking should have been welcomed. Or so I thought.

Somewhat discouraged, yet undaunted, Beth and I went ahead with the idea. We met with various consultants and in February 1994 appeared before the LAUSD Board of Education to present our idea. The board members were rather intrigued by our proposal, but the complications they raised began to seem overwhelming. Beth and I decided to try another avenue toward diversity.

I decided that if my efforts to seek a desegregated educational community couldn't happen in a public/private partnership, then I would create a private school that would accomplish the same goals. I wanted to bring together children from all racial, ethnic, economic, cultural, and national groups to study, to learn to respect each other, and to value and celebrate diversity. I remember telling my assistant, Adrienne McCandless—now the chief financial officer of New Roads School—that she and I should start a new school. We drew up some initial plans and a timetable and arranged for our first step.

The first step, in 1994, was to gather together a few colleagues from other ventures and design a nonprofit foundation dedicated to creating new schools. We named it the New Visions Foundation, and it would rest on several principles. First, we decided that any school designed by New Visions would comprise a diverse set of students and parents, teachers and administrators, and trustees and advisors, as well as a diverse curriculum. Second, our schools had to reflect a commitment to social justice and environmental sanity. To guarantee our pledge of diversity, we wrote into our bylaws a requirement that any New Visions school would consist of a minimum of 40 percent nonwhite students.

In its early years, Crossroads School had about 22 percent students of color, with about ten percent of its operating income dedicated to financial aid. While this was an exemplary commitment, our new mission was to achieve a 40 to 50 percent diversity factor.

Our new board itself represented a diverse collection of economic, social, racial, and cultural backgrounds. Nat Trives, our first board president, had served as president of the Crossroads School Board and was one of the few African American school board presidents in the country. Herbert Lucas was a board member both of the Getty Foundation and Princeton University. David Yoshimaru brought computer expertise, and Myung Lee brought leadership in the Korean community. Daniel Cano, a college teacher and Latino novelist, brought a unique community perspective, as did Hector Orci, the president of La Agencia, a Latino public-relations firm. David Newman brought expertise in nonprofit law. Karen Sperling, a children's writer and community worker, and Lori Rousso, a veteran teacher, brought wisdom and experience with children. Laura Donnelley and John Morton brought their dedication to creating community programs and new ventures, and Donzaleigh Abernathy, the daughter of Ralph Abernathy, brought to the board grace, experience, passion, and credibility. In less than twelve months, this extraordinary group was able to launch a new school: New Roads School.

Because New Roads was planning to forgo about 60 percent of its potential income as financial aid, and we had no initial funds to purchase a campus, it was clear we could not afford to put the school in a high-rent location. On the other hand, we needed to locate our campus where the 50 percent who could pay tuition of nearly $12,000 the first year would be willing to place their children. A search led us to the Boys & Girls Clubs of Santa Monica, which served primarily an after-school, public school population. Nat Trives and I met with Allen Young, one of the truly superb administrators of Boys & Girls Clubs nationally, and we pledged to raise the funds to renovate his building for school use and to lease the space from 8:00 a.m. to 3:00 p.m. Since many of our children had single mothers or two working parents, some students could attend the after-school programs of the Boys & Girls Clubs, which had an indoor gymnasium and two outdoor playgrounds.

As our first head of school, we hired David Bryan, a former lawyer and teacher as well as dean of the Human Development Department at Crossroads. David offered a rare combination of right- and left-brain intelligence, creativity, and imagination mixed with rigorous attention to detail. David embodied the values of kindness, warmth, and sensitivity to others' feelings. The school's quick success was directly attributable to him.

David immediately shared our vision for the school: a challenging academic, college-prep program, a student-centered approach, a balanced and enriched curriculum, a commitment to social justice and environmental sanity, and concern for those less fortunate. Most of all, *we wanted to radicalize our students.*

In the beginning, September 1994, the board contributed $50,000 in seed money. I was designated as the acting headmaster until July 1, 1995, when David took over. David, Adrienne, and I designed and produced a brochure, then advertised a series of open houses in twenty-two newspapers and set about recruiting a student body. I had counted on drawing most of the full-tuition-paying families from the Crossroads waiting list. The open houses went well, and we began receiving letters of inquiry and requests for applications. During this time (November through January), I mailed our brochure to more than 400 families who had applied to Crossroads, together with a return postcard requesting information, then sat back and waited for the onslaught of inquiries.

They did not come. In fact, the Crossroads waiting list proved to be a dry well. To this day, I don't quite understand why. I was shocked and even fearful. The board and I had projected a budget with forty to forty-five full-paying-equivalent students, which would underwrite a large number of families who could make only partial payments. My guess is that New Roads was simply too new, "too experimental." Furthermore, a *Los Angeles Times* article about the school stressed its "affirmative action" qualities rather than its academic goals, and this slant may have frightened away some applicants. Gradually, one by one, full-pay families did sign up. Meanwhile, we had attracted a wonderful pool of financial-aid applicants, mostly from public schools where I knew the principals, who in turn trusted me and saw the new school as a great opportunity for selected students.

We opened in September of 1995 with seventy students: 50 percent were students of color and 60 percent of students (both white and nonwhite) receiving financial aid. We had met our goal of diversity as well as our goal (if barely) of enough full-pay families. Furthermore, we had a bright, eager, talented bunch of kids.

The first year was remarkably smooth for a new school. New Visions Foundation operated a balanced budget and ran an efficient and challenging program. David took the entire school to a ranch in Tecate, Mexico, as part of a plan to provide "intensive study of Spanish." Our students were the guests of a local Mexican public school with which we developed an expanding sister-school relationship.

Some other first-year features were a required two-day-a-week martial-arts class, a rich menu of courses in the arts, and a host of after-school activities we called "school after school." Securing the enrollment balance for the second year was less of a struggle. New Roads, it seemed, was here to stay.

From the beginning, the students mixed well. After a brief initial period during which the African American girls "clustered," and four Asians who had come from the same school hung out together, race gradually diminished as the primary basis for forming friendships. Students saw a diverse board and an integrated faculty openly and freely discussing controversial issues. They began to relax and perform well in the new and inclusive atmosphere, in an environment in which respect was at the very intellectual core of the curriculum and at the soul of the institution.

The parents, however, did not come together as quickly. The realities of geographic and economic segregation and separateness worked against any real social integration of parents. Nevertheless, we found that parents did form collegial associations when they worked on projects together. As we urged white parents not to dominate certain areas in which they had more experience, such as fundraising and event design, minority families overcame their initial reluctance to participate.

At the same time, the Board of Trustees struggled to arrive at a clear, comprehensive, inclusive statement of our diversity mission. Initially, we stated that a minimum of 40 percent of students must be students of color. Then several trustees asked whether we really needed a percentage. Why couldn't New Roads just affirm its commitment to diversity and leave it at that? One board member was concerned that a future board might say that we have diversity since we have Jews, Catholics, Lutherans, Irish, Germans, and so forth, which may be diverse but also all-white.

At this time we were planning a branch of New Roads in an area named Baldwin Hills, which has a high density of African American families. One African American trustee asked whether it would still be a New Visions school if it had 90 percent black students, since there would be more than 40 percent students of color but no real diversity. Then another trustee proposed an amendment stating that no one racial group should constitute more than 60 percent. Ultimately, we affirmed our commitment to achieving a student body with a minimum of 40 percent students of color, with no group representing more than 60 percent of the total, and, ideally, with no one racial group representing a predominance.

**with Nat Trives—
partners for over 45 years**

There was one particularly poignant moment in these discussions concerning students of color. Nat Trives, the president of the New Visions Foundation, has been a friend of mine for forty years and had always been a tireless worker for a better society, always trying to bring people together, to create community, harmony, and cooperation. I heard a genuine sense of pain and disappointment in his voice when he said, "You know, I have had the education, the skills, the knowledge to reach certain levels of power and responsibility in our society, but I have lacked one thing that has held me back and, frankly, it has been devastating: I have lacked skin privilege." The room fell silent for a moment. I felt closer to Nat at a deeper level than ever before.

The board decided to invest a $150,000 faculty endowment grant from the Ahmanson Foundation in a mutual fund dedicated to investing in socially responsible corporations. The board felt that wherever possible, schools need to lead, not just follow.

New Roads concluded its second year in June of 1997. The school then had four grades (six through nine) and a total enrollment of 115 students. The eighth grade insisted on a culmination (graduation) ceremony, which we held in a rustic setting. It was virtually an old-fashioned "love-in" with parents, teachers, students, trustees, and administrators praising the school's vision, achievements, and—perhaps its most compelling ingredient—hope. The school community believed it was breaking down stereotypes and showing that rich and poor, as well as racially, ethnically, and culturally diverse student bodies and their families could work together in harmony and mutual respect.

Perhaps I should have learned my lesson from the experience at Coeur d'Alene, but in seeking a new campus I ventured again into the public school/private school, joint-venture arena. My idea was to utilize underused public school space for the mutual benefit of a public school and a private school. I approached a local public elementary school principal, Yuri Hayashi, who administered Walgrove Avenue Elementary School, a campus of ten-plus acres in West Los Angeles, about seven acres of them unused, cracked, weed-infested asphalt. My idea was that New Roads would enter into a long-term (fifty-year) lease with the Los Angeles Unified School District and build our high school on the back one-third of the property. The idea, however, proved too difficult for LAUSD to accept, so after six months of negotiations, I dropped the idea.

But as the enrollment grew, so did our challenges. On July 1, 1999, I received a telephone call from David Bryan, who said, "Paul, it's not that I'm panicking, but we have a ninth-through eleventh-grade group of parents and students who want to know where—and even if—the high school is going to be in September." We still had not secured a site that was adequate for our students. I mumbled something about not worrying and us finding something, but I also was in a state of high anxiety. Fortunately, I had heard via the grapevine that another private school was moving out of a prime location. We called the landlord, and at the eleventh hour on

July 30, 1999, we were able to sign a lease for a small campus: one U-shaped building (formerly called Hot Tub Fever) surrounding a tiny courtyard in an increasingly popular and valuable commercial corridor on Olympic Boulevard in West Los Angeles. Having dodged the bullet, we had twenty-seven days to get ready for our ninth-, tenth-, and eleventh-grade students to arrive.

Typically, when families from underserved neighborhoods seek a high-quality college-preparatory private school for their children, they must trek across town to higher-income neighborhoods, where the "white folks" have established elitist schools. The New Visions Foundation decided to establish a second high-quality private school, this time in a predominantly African American neighborhood. We hoped our school's reputation would also attract white, Latino, and Asian families.

In searching for that campus, we focused on Baldwin Hills, an economically diverse minority neighborhood that consists primarily of African American families. We heard of a Baha'i temple that was planning to remodel one wing of its building into a community center. We met with the personnel there and suggested that they remodel the space into a school for grades six through eight and rent it to us during the day. After 6:00 p.m., they could use the space for their community center. They agreed and once again we entered into a shared-use agreement that we hoped would be a win–win program for each organization.

To my great disappointment, the Baldwin Hills campus failed for financial reasons. Ironically, it was a big educational success—parents, teachers, and students saw the school campus as a jewel. It had small classes, high morale, wonderful teachers, and parents who saw their children—many for the first time—loving school and fully engaged in the process.

When we launched this private school in a predominantly black neighborhood, I believed that we could attract upper-middle-class and upper-class African Americans as well as whites from surrounding vicinities—some of whom would be able to pay from half to full tuition. We did not attract any! Those who could pay continued to send their children across town to existing prestigious, predominantly white schools rather than taking a chance on a brand-new school in their own neighborhood. Perhaps these families were looking us over to see whether we would survive and flourish. But while they waited—if in fact, they were waiting—we lost money: more than $1.5 million after five years. At the end of the fourth year, we had to face reality: the school had exactly the same enrollment of fifty-two students as the first year. Of the fifty-two students, only two paid full tuition. Consequently, the Board of Trustees voted to close the campus at the end of the fifth year, when our lease expired at the Baha'i temple. I realized after the fact that we had miscalculated.

We had erred in trying to impose an idealistic vision upon the community without a strong base of support to launch the school. We launched it first, then tried to persuade the community to join us. When I later helped create a charter school in a low-income neighborhood, it succeeded because the community had invited us.

Postscript

Our fully integrated New Roads School works. The diversity we intentionally cultivated from our board of directors and faculty to our student body—has helped create a wonderful community where differences are respected and honored. In addition to its commitment to diversity, New Roads School seeks to imbue its students with a passion for social justice. From the very names of world leaders and heroes on the classroom doors (as at Crossroads, we don't give rooms numbers, but instead name them after such figures as Zapata, Menchu, Aung San Suu Kyi, Huerta, Chomsky, Chavez, etc.) to the weekly workshops on social justice and environmental issues, New Roads holds true to its founding philosophy. The workshops are perhaps the curricular key to this quest. In each workshop—a weekly two-hour class team-taught by three or four teachers—students are engaged in discussions, activities, and projects dealing with issues such as prejudice, rights of the disabled, endangered species, child labor, animal rights, using art in activism, AIDS, ecological design, consumerism, and the dynamics between poverty and privilege.

The essence of the workshops is to bring issues to students' consciousness and to activate their inherent sense of fairness. The theory behind the workshops is that service and the desire to take action would grow out of an ongoing exploration of an issue. For example, issues of huge global disparities of wealth among individuals and nations will often lead students to ask the all-important questions of *Why?* and *What can be done about this?*

Similarly, the school determined to arouse students' curiosity, interest, and ultimately indignation about the rapid eco-depletion of their heritage, the Earth, by the forces of consumerism and corporate profit. The workshops on ecology and environmental sanity are designed not to frighten students but to help them learn to care and to seek ways in their lives to undo damage and to prevent further degradation of our beautiful planet and all its unique resources and beauties. The administration and the faculty bring enormous energy and excitement to these workshops.

One plan at New Roads was to create a community-action major in the high school. Students in academic classes were also teaching assistants in some workshop classes, and they helped organize the workshop days. In addition, high school students created workshop presentations for middle school students.

It is my hope that out of this curriculum, students will grow up to become progressive activists in their communities; to enter politics, social services, the arts; to work for social and economic justice and environmental sustainability—in short, to envision and commit to building a more sane, rational, and compassionate society. That is New Roads School's vision and mission.

CHAPTER 22

A Home for New Roads School and the Herb Alpert Educational Village

Obstacles are those frightful things you see
when you take your eyes off the goal.

—Hannah More

QUESTION: HOW DO YOU BUY 2.7 acres of prime West Los Angeles real estate to create a campus for a school that has no funds in the bank and no endowment?

Answer: You pour a heavy dose of chutzpah into a gallon of hope and stir with your lucky wand.

As of August 1999 New Roads School occupied the 2,000-square-foot former Hot Tub Fever building in Santa Monica. Soon afterward, we secured a lease for a second building next door and raised a chunk of money to remodel it. But almost as soon as New Roads School moved in, I noticed developers sniffing around, so I approached the owners of the property to discuss our own peremptory purchase. My reputation, and a bit of braggadocio feigned for the meetings, convinced them that we were serious potential buyers.

To make a very long and complicated story short, in late December of 1999 (with $250,000 applied toward the purchase), New Visions Foundation opened escrow to purchase 1.25 acres of a 2.7-acre parcel fronting on Olympic Boulevard. I now had sixty days to find a down payment of $2.5 million cash toward the $6.5 million purchase. No sooner did we raise the funds than the second half of the parcel (1.5 acres) was offered to New Visions Foundation for an additional $7.15 million. Since we didn't have the money to buy the first parcel, I decided to use the money we didn't have to go after the second parcel, applying the same resources of chutzpah mixed with hope, along with the assumption that luck would magically be provided.

Fortunately, with help from many of the same people, notably Herb Alpert, Lee Walcott of the Ahmanson Foundation, and Fred Ali of the Weingart Foundation, we managed to cobble together a purchase by December of 2000.

Thus, at the end of September 2000, New Visions Foundation—acting on behalf of New Roads School—owned two and a half acres of prime Westside real estate and had the dubious distinction of a $10.5 million debt to finance. In truth, I remember waking up in a cold sweat one evening—shortly after closing escrow on both lots—*My God*, I said to myself, *what have I done?* In my excitement and labor over buying the land, I had omitted one key ingredient—how was I going to service the debt? As New Roads was a small school with 40 percent of potential tuition income forgiven in the form of financial aid, the burden of the debt service fell upon our foundation.

The first year of servicing the $90,000-per-month debt was a time of high anxiety. Each month was a harrowing adventure in fundraising. In fact, I didn't see how I could keep going. God, they say, protects fools and drunks. Lefty Gomez once said, "I'd rather be lucky than good." Well, since I was not a drunk, I guess I was a lucky fool. A wonderful benefactor miraculously appeared offering to cover twelve months of our shortfall: $75,000 a month, or $900,000. He had read an article about New Roads and asked me to show him the school, and, being impressed by our mission, decided to support us. Initially he gave us two gifts of $50,000, but when he learned of our debt-service crisis, he decided to help in a big way. His gift gave us time to bring the mortgage, and hence the monthly payments, down.

Even though my attempts at collaboration with LAUSD were shot down twice, I still believed in the power of partnerships. I believe that a certain energy and excitement is generated by people of good will who sit in a circle and dream together. I suppose if the truth be told, I was infected years ago by the Camelot myth, the idea of the Knights of the Round Table united with a common cause. The words from the Lerner song and its association with the thousand days of JFK have haunted me for decades now:

Don't let it be forgot
That once there was a spot
For one brief shining moment
That was known as Camelot.

The idea of bringing together a group of nonprofits under one roof, with adjacent offices, a common conference room and coffee gathering place, and a theater—such a group, with similar missions of social justice, educational reform, and environmental sustainability, is at the core of the village dream. Our mantra would be "to incubate innovative ideas for export." My hope is that these ideas will have a genuine impact where they are most needed—in the education of the most underserved and highly at-risk children and youth, and also in raising public consciousness about environmental sustainability and economic and social injustice.

During this time an idea that I had earlier tried to apply to another parcel of land resurfaced. My idea was to create an "educational village": that is, to have several entities share the land and costs and to collaborate on educational projects wherever possible. I discussed the idea with a dozen or so potential partners, and gradually a plan emerged to have this village contain New Roads School, one or two other schools, and offices for the New Visions Foundation, as well as offices for ten to twelve other nonprofit organizations dedicated to social and educational justice and environmental sanity.

I brought the idea to Herb Alpert, who became equally enthusiastic. As we developed plans, Herb continued to help bring the mortgage down—from $10 million to $7 million to $4 million, with others providing substantial gifts, including a purchase completion grant of $1.5 million from the Annenberg Foundation. Thus, we were able in less than six years to eliminate the mortgage altogether: from $13.6 million to zero.

At that point, New Visions and New Roads decided not to partner with an outside entity. We determined to have the village meet the needs of New Roads School, provide for New Visions Foundation, and provide offices for ten to twelve other nonprofits. There would be a 350-seat theater for all to use, as well as a 2,000-square-foot Leadership Center with a small kitchen/coffee bar, allowing for luncheons, conferences, lectures, workshops, recitals, and the like.

Herb agreed to honor us by having the village be named the Herb Alpert Educational Village. This village would fulfill our desire to incubate innovative ideas for New Roads, the city, and hopefully, the nation. We believed that if creative, active people worked in the same building and rubbed elbows in their own coffee house, ideas would percolate, and exciting outcomes would result.

CHAPTER 23

An Elementary School for New Roads
and Charter Schools

Tell me, what is it you plan to do
with your one wild and precious life?

—Mary Oliver

Vision is the art of seeing things invisible.

—Jonathan Swift

An Elementary School for New Roads

THE ADDITION OF AN ELEMENTARY school for New Roads came about curiously. It began with Eve Weiss, the president of the board of Newbridge, a nearby private school, asking to meet with me. Newbridge had come into being a year or two after Crossroads in the early 1970s. It had done nicely for a while, but it ultimately fell on hard times. After its founder, Mike Jacobson, died in March of 2000, it was teetering on the verge of bankruptcy.

Eve asked me what to do. I told her I would help her find a leader. Serendipitously, in May of 2001, I met Patrick McCabe. He had been a successful businessman and now wanted to become involved in education. Pat and I felt an immediate bond—for one thing, we had both been captains of the Harvard School (now Harvard-Westlake) basketball team—he, nineteen years after me. Pat is a "larger-than-life" man with a passion for educating children and young people. His enthusiasm is contagious. I told him about Newbridge and suggested that he take it over and try to save it. The Newbridge board interviewed him, and on July 1, 2001, he took over the school.

Within two years, Pat raised the funds to pay off Newbridge's $300,000 debt, build the enrollment, and restore credibility to the school. This having been achieved, Pat, David Bryan, and I worked out a plan whereby Newbridge would be absorbed into New Roads School. Hence, in just under fifteen years, New Roads became a K–12 school operating on four campuses: the K–5 former Newbridge campus in a Santa Monica church; the middle school campus sharing space with the Boys & Girls Clubs; a Malibu middle school campus; and the "Hot Tub Fever" high school site.

Camino Nuevo

About the time I began to plan my summer vacation in June of 1998, at age sixty and with both daughters graduated from college (Anna from Stanford in 1995 and Emily from Northwestern in 1998), I spoke to my college roommate and still-close friend John, who asked me when I was going to retire. I responded, "I hope not for a long time." I suppose my identity by then was so tied up in being an educator that I imagined I'd wither away without a new project. Probably, as it is for my wife and for my mentor Herbert Zipper, my work is my play.

Gradually during this time, with almost daily insights and sharper vision, I came to see the crippling and often tragic growing divide between rich and poor and the increasing marginalization of poor children and youth. While rereading Jonathan Kozol's article "Still Separate, Still Unequal," I was struck almost as if by lightning by a quote from British writer Marina Warner, who said, "Well, in America you have 'the expensive children and the cheap children.'" I cannot imagine anyone not wincing and feeling instant shame that we allow such a tragedy to occur in our wealthy country. For whatever reasons, my realization—accompanied by first-hand observations—will not allow me to retire. The consigning of innocent children to the ash heaps of our society keeps me in a controlled state of outrage and stokes a desire to do something about it. Retirement is simply out of the question.

Nevertheless, with my sixty-first birthday coming up, I did begin to think of departing from Crossroads School and further exploring my work with lower-income students and schools. Almost on cue, I received a call that summer from Philip Lance, and without realizing it, I began my foray into the world of charter schools.

The foray really began on July 15, 1998, when I met Philip, an Episcopal minister with a boyish smile, piercing light-blue eyes, and a self-confident, honest manner. Philip had left an assistant rector position at a wealthy Beverly Hills parish and had begun working in the low-income MacArthur Park neighborhood. First he created a storefront church, then a thrift shop for parishioners, and then a profit-sharing maintenance company. His parish consisted mainly of Latinos, many undocumented, some just out of jail or on probation, as well as drug users, gang members, unemployed men and women, single moms, all with a long list of troubles. When Philip's parishioners told him that their children were getting a poor education in the local public schools, he said he would try to help. Someone suggested that he speak to me.

At our initial meeting, I suggested that he and I should look into the relatively new phenomenon of charter schools. We wound up creating a three-way collaboration among Philip's nonprofit Pueblo Nuevo Development Corporation, New Visions Foundation, and ExED, a nonprofit organization specializing in charter-school management. Philip, representing PNDC, would be the liaison with the community, New Visions would design the curriculum, and ExED would administer the business side of things.

We decided that this school would be located in a two-story mini-mall in the neighborhood. It had underground parking, a courtyard that could be used for play, and nearly completed offices that could be divided into classrooms. We set out immediately to raise $2 million to buy the property and remodel it into a beautiful structure. I also suggested the name—a New Roads clone—Camino Nuevo.

So in relatively short order—about twenty-six months—we secured a charter; bought and remodeled a mini-mall; hired a principal, faculty, and staff; created a 501(c)(3) nonprofit organization; and put together a board. In September of 2000 we opened the school, Camino Nuevo Charter Academy. We had some stumbles in the first two years, but under the leadership of Executive Director Ana Ponce, the school quickly began to flourish. Camino now has seven campuses, and its test scores are in the top 10 percent of all similar schools in California.

Los Angeles Academy of Arts and Enterprise (LAAAE)
In June 2005—having launched P.S. Arts in 1993, New Roads School in 1994–95, Camino Nuevo Charter Academy in 2000, and an education program at Camp Gonzales, a probation camp in 2001—my plate seemed full. I was on three separate boards and not looking for any more work. I was also writing more. My book on Herbert Zipper, *Dachau Song*, was published in 1992; a book on education, *For Mortal Stakes* appeared in 1998; a collection of poems, *A Postcard from Bali*, in 2002; and a second book on education, *Proceed with Passion*, was published in 2004. All the while, I was writing a column in the *Santa Monica Mirror*—often what a friend called "Paul's liberal whining."

Consequently, I was at first hesitant when I received a call in 2005 from a noted filmmaker, Moctesuma Esparza. Mocte, as his friends call him, wanted to start a charter school for Mexican-American and other Latino children with a curricular emphasis on the arts and enterprise. He had heard of me and my propensity for starting new schools. Mocte and I met with Hector Orci, the head of an excellent Latino public relations firm, and the three of us decided to work together. We quickly hit upon the name: Los Angeles Academy of Arts and Enterprise (LAAAE).

Again, we set up a triangular model with Mocte as liaison to the community, New Visions Foundation providing the educational and arts vision, and ExED managing business operations. We found a church in the mid-Wilshire area to house the school, and in 2006 LAAAE opened its doors to sixth-, seventh-, and eighth-grade students. Now in its eighth year, LAAAE occupies a campus it is seeking to buy. Its first senior class graduated in 2012.

New Village Girls Academy

After Camino Nuevo and LAAAE, a third charter collaboration offer presented itself. I received a call from an attorney named Andy Bogen, who had been a lawyer at Gibson, Dunn & Crutcher for more than forty-one years and was also chairman of the board at St. Anne's, a residential treatment center for pregnant girls and teenage mothers. Andy is a man dedicated to social justice and to helping those most in need. His vision was to start a high school (grades 9-12) for some of the girls from the treatment center on St. Anne's property in West Hollywood. On the property was a run-down, underused school building LAUSD leased as a center for independent-studies students.

Andy's idea was to create a charter school that could serve some of the girls from St. Anne's as well as neighborhood girls. He asked whether I would help. This was a radical idea in the sense that while Andy would do the lion's share of the fundraising, my involvement would add credibility to the project and help secure foundation grants. In addition, New Visions pledged to write the curriculum piece of the charter proposal, which was in turn approved by LAUSD (the Los Angeles Unified School District). I couldn't say no. Within nine months, by September of 2006, the school opened as New Village Charter High School (it was recently renamed New Village Girls Academy). Basically the approach was to treat each girl as an individual project. The arts and Council, I believed, would be avenues for engaging the girls.

Again, after a few stumbles and some personnel changes and problems, the school has gradually made progress. Initially, two New Visions Foundation employees, Kelly Kagan and Julianna Coco, were enormously resourceful and wise in dealing with these challenged girls. I must say these girls were the toughest bunch of students I had ever encountered. They had been victims of sexual and parental abuse, rape, and fragmented and dysfunctional families; many were foster children and/or on probation, and many were from two to several grade levels behind academically, with spotty, incomplete, and even inaccurate transcripts. And, at ages fourteen and fifteen, many were mothers. But we discovered that such girls can overcome their pasts, they can become engaged in vocational or academic learning, and they can go to college with positive attitudes.

For example, the following statistics described the 2012-13 student body:

100% qualified for free or reduced lunch
45% pregnant and/or parenting
13% foster-care youth
33% English Language Learners
10% probation youth
40% two or more years behind in credits

Yet remarkably, in 2012, the number of students accepted by 4-year colleges improved by 250% over any other year, to 13 of the 31 graduates. And of the 2011 graduates that entered two and four-year colleges, 17 completed one year of college, and from those, 11 have completed more than one year.

What we've learned is that these young women can take charge of their lives. They do, however, need outside-the-box programs and support.

CHAPTER 24

Fostering Success:
Quality Education for Foster Children and Youth

The test of the morality of a society
is what it does for its children.

—Dietrich Bonhoeffer

IN EARLY 2000 A MUTUAL friend arranged a meeting for me with a foster care advocate, Deanne Shartin. Deanne had been asked to set up a meeting with me and philanthropist Peter Morton, who had offered to provide a few scholarships for foster children to attend private schools and wanted me to arrange one at Crossroads. As it turned out, the deadline at Crossroads had passed, but we were able to place five students among New Roads, Archer, and Marlborough (the latter two are girls' schools in Los Angeles).

Prior to the lunch, I learned that of our nation's 500,000 foster youth, only 2 percent graduate from college. The rest would likely face unemployment, incarceration, dependence on public assistance, homelessness, substance abuse, emotional and psychological deprivation, nonmarital childbirth, and the whole sorry list of dismal statistics associated with foster youth and adults.

All of this was rather new to me and fed my growing sense of disgust with yet another example of our society's inexcusable treatment of innocent and deprived children and youth. Again, it seemed as though I could at least do something. That something manifested itself rather quickly. After placing the first of the initial five foster youths in private schools, we saw rather startling results: all five students were flourishing for the first time in their lives. In time, all five graduated from high school and went to prestigious colleges. These five were, by the way, not specially selected "cream-of-the-crop" students. One, for example, entered her private school ninth grade having attended sixteen previous schools.

I was so surprised by the first-year success of these students that an idea presented itself to me: I asked Deanne whether she would come to work full-time for New Visions Foundation so we could start a program placing foster students in independent schools. She agreed, and I found a sponsor to cover her salary.

And so began the Center for Educational Opportunity, under the umbrella of New Visions Foundation. In this program, we first identify—with recommendations from social-service agencies and social workers—youth who might be able to handle the demands of a private school. Then we meet with the students and their foster parents to explain the potential benefits of attending an independent school. If the student and his or her foster parents agree, we then approach the heads of nearby private schools and make the match. The first five students received tuition payments from the Peter Morton grant. Since then, as the program has grown, we ask the private schools to provide their own full scholarships for these students. Our current program director, Tiffany Shirley, stays in touch with the students to make sure that all is going well.

Our foster program was one of those good ideas that actually worked. First and foremost, it stabilized the lives of these students. Once enrolled in a high-quality school, they stayed. They stopped moving from school to school and from foster home to foster home—some had moved as often as ten or fifteen times before the ninth grade. At the end of our first year, all five placements were flourishing, so we went to fourteen in the second year, with the same positive results.

Moreover, these students caught up quickly. They survived, even in some of the most demanding private schools in town. They needed tutoring, remedial work, hand-holding, and encouragement, but they learned they could do it. An extraordinary 95 percent stayed at one school and graduated.

Being surrounded by high school students who were talking about what college they would be attending led our placements to join in. Remarkably, our first four graduates from college earned their degrees at MIT, Skidmore, Brown, and Tufts (cum laude). As of 2014 there are forty-five elementary through middle- and high-school students (K-12), with *eight* seniors, all graduating; and *forty-six* college students. We have *eleven* incoming students who will begin attending their new schools this fall.

A final byproduct of the program was that foster parents began to see their foster charges with new respect. They saw children coming alive to school and education, students making plans for college, and better-behaved and more motivated students. It was a win-win situation.

What I keep learning, the more I engage in low-income social and educational arenas and issues, is how narrow my own awareness of inclusion and deprivation has been. For example, I had not realized how alone foster youth are—not just when they are taken from their families and placed in a foster home, or a series of homes, but when they are bounced from school to school. Of course, that aloneness is most extreme when at age eighteen, they "age out" of their foster home and are in effect homeless. I hadn't known any of this because I never encountered it.

Meeting these young people, however, and hearing their stories opened my eyes and my heart. I was also introduced to Andrew Bridge, and as we became friends, he showed me a manuscript of his life story. *Hope's Boy* gave me a detailed account of the foster world. Andrew has made an amazing success of his life. He is, however, exceptional. The statistics surrounding foster youth are not at all encouraging.

What does encourage me is my growing awareness of how a quality education can transform lives. I keep coming back to the same set of conclusions regarding so-called "at-risk" children and youth. We, society, our nation put them at-risk because we fail them. We give the least advantaged the most substandard schools to attend. They are at-risk primarily because they are not provided with the same opportunities that well-to-do families provide their children. In the United States, we do in fact have, as Warner fittingly said, "expensive children and cheap children."

I do not know why we are so short on compassion in the United States, but for reasons I cannot fully grasp myself, I do know that it infuriates me. It seems so unfair. Why we have such a hard time providing a just and fair society eludes me.

We have made a discovery in our foster program, perhaps not original or terribly surprising: as a society, we set the bar too low. Foster youth can make it into college, do well, and graduate. Like all underserved children and youth, they need support and encouragement, but they can do it. They can, in fact, do it very well.

CHAPTER 25

Camp Gonzales:
Into the Thickets of Juvenile Justice

I went from courthouse knowledge
to Morehouse College.

—Alton Pitre

Something there is that doesn't love a wall . . .

—Robert Frost, "Mending Wall"

SOMETIME IN 2001 I RECEIVED a phone call from a relative stranger named Carol
Biondi. Carol was a friend of a Crossroads parent, Jo Kaplan, and both were deeply
involved in the juvenile justice system. Specifically, Carol and Jo were passionate
supporters and benefactors of Camp Gonzales, a probation camp in Southern California for incarcerated boys from fourteen to eighteen years old. Camp Gonzales
lies high in the mountains above Pepperdine University in Malibu.

Carol was concerned about the education being provided at Camp Gonzales.
She asked me to look it over and tell her what I thought. Little aware of the implica-
tions of saying "yes," I went up to Camp Gonzales on a couple of occasions and interviewed probation officers, the camp director, and the school administrator. The
boys took classes provided by the Los Angeles County Office of Education every
day from 8:00 a.m. to 3:00 p.m. Of course, I interviewed several boys, individually
and in small groups. A pretty clear picture emerged rather quickly.

"So, what do you think?" Carol inquired.

"Well," I responded, "first of all, the boys are not interviewed when they arrive at the camp, so no one finds out whether they have any interests to build upon during their three, six, or nine months of being locked up. Second, they're not educated very well while they are there. Third, they are not placed anywhere when they're released, so, of course, they drift back into their neighborhoods and rejoin their gangs. Most recidivate to even higher levels of incarceration and serve longer sentences. Other than that, it's a great system."

"What would you do to correct this?" she asked. I answered that I would attack on all three fronts. "Good," she said. "I will get you a grant." And she did. True to her word, Carol got us a five-year grant, and we have been involved with Camp Gonzales ever since. In fact, we received a five-year extension of our contract in 2013.

One of the key principles I try to implement in any new venture is to provide low-income students with the quality of education they would receive at a first-rate private school. When Carol asked me to design a plan to improve the education at Camp Gonzales, I was guided by this thought.

Since the Los Angeles County Office of Education controlled the boys' education at Camp Gonzales from 8:00 a.m. to 3:00 p.m., I suggested that we initiate a Camp Partners program to offer after-school electives from 3:00 p.m. to dinner (usually pretty much a "nothing-to-do" time at the camp). These electives would include film-making, creative writing, poetry and rap, theater writing, acting and scene productions, music-synthesizer playing, computer skills, journalism (Camp Gonzales has a student-produced newspaper), GED preparation, and life-skills classes. The idea was to excite the boys, reward them for positive self-expression, gain their trust, and show them—often for the first time—that education can be enjoyable.

Once, during an early visit to the camp, I sat in a circle with a group of boys and asked them what they liked to do when on their own. We went around the circle—"hang out with friends," "listen to music," etc.—then one of them said to me, "What do you like to do, man?"

I said, "Sometimes shoot hoops, sometimes write poetry." Not much response. Later, as I was leaving the camp and just about to go through the metal detectors, I felt something being shoved into my back pocket by a big, tough-looking, tattooed Latino boy. He looked around nervously and then whispered, "I write poetry too."

Flash forward a few years to what had become our annual holiday party for the boys. As usual, Carol Biondi arranged for an In-N-Out Burger truck to come into the camp, we gave each boy a gift, and we had a lunch-assembly where a few adults spoke, but mostly the boys performed. A highlight had become their reading of their own poetry with the other boys cheering their work. Clearly, I can proudly say that we had changed the culture in the camp.

Beyond this one anecdote are dozens more: boys in college, boys we have placed in private high schools, jobs we have secured for them—three boys are now interns at New Visions Foundation—and long-term (three to five years) post-camp relationships that our director, Fernando Rodriguez, counselors, and teachers have forged with them.

My encounters, friendships, and observations of these boys have taught me many things, but primarily my deep beliefs have been reinforced and confirmed: these boys were innocent and unspoiled at birth. As babies, they were a source of hope for the future in their families. Their current state of incarceration mostly was the result of a hostile, un-nurturing environment in a country that now writes off its inner-city kids as "throw-aways." But show them interest, a little bit of affection and encouragement, offer them exciting classes, allow them opportunities for saying something positive about their inner world, and guess what? They respond. They grow. They develop positive goals. They begin to see that a decent future might just be possible.

For the most part, these boys don't want lives of violence, they don't want to die, and they don't want to wind up as useless junkies or fathers who can't care for their children. They want something better than that, and to my joy and pride, we have been able to make some of this happen at Camp Gonzales and beyond.

The "beyond" part is critical. Redirecting lives is not an overnight event. It often takes years, and it comes about because someone—a teacher, a counselor, a mentor, a probation officer—cares enough to stay involved, to be there when the inevitable setbacks occur, to believe in a young man or woman. Relationship is key. But hasn't this always been so? I know that all my years as an educator and education reformer have convinced me that we as a country sell our youth way short. It need not be so. For me, Jonathan Kozol's words echo again: "We soil them [our youth] needlessly."

CHAPTER 26

The Herb Alpert Educational Village and the Coalition for Engaged Education

The trick is to keep your heart open.
You got to listen wit' your heart.
That's the trick.

—Walter Mosley, *Fearless Jones*

By 2006, WE HAD COMPLETELY paid off the purchase of the 2.7 acres of land on Olympic Boulevard—$13.6 million, not including interest along the way. So we then set our sights on a new campus for New Roads School and a home for the New Visions Foundation. The plans called for a three-phase construction project with Phase 1 to cost $24 million. New Roads raised $2 million, and New Visions Foundation raised $9 million. In addition, a $13 million bond was secured from California Bank & Trust. Construction commenced in October of 2010. Construction was completed in November of 2012. The first 30,000-square-foot building— The Capshaw-Spielberg Center for Art and Educational Justice—houses the Ann and Jerry Moss Theater (343 seats); New Visions, which focuses on educational reform and facilitates Engaged Education for at-risk children and youth, including those in the foster system, juvenile justice arena, and those who are economically disadvantaged; a leadership/conference center; offices for twelve other nonprofits; and classrooms for New Roads School.

Those are the facts. In reality, this project has been the most difficult and frustrating experience of my professional life, reducing me, on numerous occasions, to near despair. The difficulty of securing major donors and then requesting their patience as construction met delay after delay, the struggles to secure a bank loan, and the constant feeling that the fundraising was primarily my responsibility caused me sleepless nights. I walked around my house wondering whether I had entangled New Visions in a morass from which we could not escape. I found myself considering whether I had fallen into the trap of overexpansion mixed with hubris that had ensnared my father and led him into Chapter 11. Was I truly my father's son?

Fortunately, through all this, Herb Alpert never wavered in his support and personal faith in me. Without this reassurance, I don't think that I would have been able to keep the project on track.

Our shining moment occurred on March 24, 2013, when the Herb Alpert Educational Village was opened in the theater named after Herb's former partner, Jerry Moss. Herb and his wife Lani Hall, a truly great singer, were to give the opening concert. Lani developed laryngitis and couldn't perform, so Herb and his jazz trio put together a stunning program. David Bryan introduced me, and I walked out on stage to receive a surprising and heart-warming standing ovation. (I nodded to Mary Ann, seated in the front of the theater, commenting that it would be nice to receive such a welcome when I came home from work after each day.) I then introduced Herb, and I believe both of us were deeply touched by the moment. If the fates permit, it won't be my final effort at pulling off a major piece of construction, but it was a huge relief after thirteen years of a difficult project.

Another shining moment occurred on July 16 of 2014, when seventy probation officers came to the Moss Theater for an all-day professional-growth training. Many came reluctantly and skeptically, for the day was billed as a day of arts and human development experiences. Our plan was to provide the probation officers with some of what we provide the incarcerated youth: poetry and journal writing, improvisational theater games, drumming—ways to both go deeper inward and to express the self and connect more genuinely with others. By the end of the day, there was a remarkable shift in the air. Many came to see why what we do with the youth works, why it is so crucial.

Now, after over a year and a half, the Moss Theater is a smashing success with New Roads, Coalition for Engaged Education (our new name), the Village Partners, and the public at large using it to the maximum. The acoustics designed by Yasu Toyota (who consulted on Disney Hall) work well for all forms of performance and presentation—vocal, instrumental, film, etc. After ten years of giving birth to this village, I not only enjoy it but am eager to help make it a vibrant and innovative place for education reform. Now, as I walk up the stairs to my third-story office, I feel a wonderful mixture of relief, pride, and simple well-being.

CHAPTER 27

LENZ:
The Lennox Educational Neighborhood Zone

To be hopeful in bad times is not just foolishly romantic, it is based
on the fact that human history is a history of not only cruelty but
also of compassion, sacrifice, courage, kindness. What we choose to
emphasize in this complex history will determine our lives.

—Howard Zinn

NESTLED BETWEEN TWO FREEWAYS AND two major boulevards, directly under
the flight approaches of planes landing every two minutes at LAX, sits the unincorporated town of Lennox. Unknown even to most Angelinos, Lennox is densely
populated—24,000 people within a 1.3-square-mile area—and it possesses one of
the highest poverty rates in California. Lennox is 95 percent Latino and has high
rates of domestic violence, transience, unemployment, homelessness, and gang activity, as well as a large number of undocumented immigrants. English is spoken in
virtually none of the households.

The Lennox school district (K–8) includes over 10,000 students. There are five
elementary schools that feed into one large middle school with two small charter
high schools that are able to absorb only about 50 percent of graduating eighth-
graders. The other 50 percent pretty much evaporate and contribute to the esti-
mated 65 percent dropout rate in the district.

I have learned a great deal about Lennox from my daughter, Emily, who has been a counselor at one of the five elementary schools for the last ten years. She encounters every social, cultural, and behavioral problem anyone could imagine. Much of it is heartbreaking. These children are born into enormous disadvantages, and for many the future is bleak indeed.

One day Emily asked me, "Dad, have you ever heard of Geoffrey Canada?"

I replied, "Of course. He's a sort of an urban hero who founded the Harlem Children's Zone."

She continued, "Well, what do you think about a 'Harlem Children's Zone' model for Lennox?"

"Great idea," I said, and for the last four years at Coalition for Engaged Education, we have been developing such a program.

When I visit classes, attend community meetings, or just drive around Lennox, I am filled with the same feelings of sadness that I had as a child growing up in a wealthy neighborhood with various minorities acting in servant and service roles in our home and in neighboring homes. I believe we have progressed very little over the centuries in organizing the planet so that everyone can share its vast resources. It is still true in America that if you are born poor, you are pretty much doomed to stay poor. The exceptions are just that. I keep hoping that someday our country will realize that with modest adjustments in the distribution of wealth and opportunity, each American adult and child could find a level of decency and equity.

Our plan at Coalition for Engaged Education is to try, in partnership with the Lennox School District through our program called LENZ (the Lennox Educational Neighborhood Zone), to raise both the quality of education in the school district as well as the quality of life in the surrounding neighborhood. In fact, I am convinced that the two are inextricably bound. For a child who comes from a home where English is not spoken; where neither parent graduated from high school, let alone college; where the father, here legally or illegally, is unemployed; where frustrated fathers often beat their wives and/or their children; where there are no books in the home; where two or three families are sharing a one- or two-bedroom house; where proper nutrition is scant and, hence, 40 percent of children are classified as obese by the third grade; where the block is not safe; and on and on—the obstacles to receiving a college-preparatory education are immense. Social, health, economic issues are so devastating that each child and each school is forced to try to play "catch-up" from age two onward!

Our goal is to attack on two fronts simultaneously: First, to assist the Lennox School District with the daily in-school, after-school, and summer academic programs, and with adding the arts and human development as well as environmental and athletic programs. Second, to provide a variety of wraparound social, health, and economic services. The challenges are enormous, not the least of which is additional fundraising.

Because about one-third of Lennox students have no high school to attend when they become ninth-graders, one of our goals is to create a new high school campus, which will focus on the arts. Given my love of and experience with arts education, I am eager to help design such a project. This would be the sixth and probably last school I will have directly helped to create.

My vision of such a school is one that has a beautiful theater, which will also serve as a community resource. Various film series can be shown for both children and adults. There can be guest dance and theater performances, Lennox parent performing groups, and also some visiting celebrity performances. The adults who live in Lennox have expressed a genuine passion for such arts programs. While we are seeking a major donor to achieve a dramatic, high impact set of programs for Lennox, we have instituted two extraordinary programs which—although not district wide—have changed lives.

My daughter Emily has worked in Lennox for ten years as a school counselor, dealing often with heartbreaking cases of traumatized children. These children are victims of the worst kind of experiences. Without specific and long-term counseling, they cannot learn and succeed. To that end, we raised funds to create a trauma center—JUNTOS—in partnership with UCLA, Echo Parenting, and other entities. In its two years, it has served a total of 623 individual children and their family members. In fact, JUNTOS has become so successful it has incorporated as a separate nonprofit organization, under Emily's direction.

A second program began in the summer of 2013. In April, we identified twenty Lennox middle-school students who had not signed up for ninth grade and were pretty much headed toward gangs and drop-out status. Kelly Kagan Law, our Vice President, and Liz Nolan, a Crossroads graduate and a new hire at the Coalition for Engaged Education, and I designed a comprehensive, experiential, focused, six-week summer program for these twenty students and provided them with every positive experience we could in those six weeks: arts classes, music, drumming, poetry writing, counseling and individual mentoring, field trips to places they had never before visited, such as the Pacific Ocean, downtown Los Angeles, local museums, et cetera. In short, we gave them enrichment, individual care, and encouragement. Also, we spent one-sixth of a private-school tuition for this program, that is $5,000 per pupil for the six weeks. This level of expenditure, if we extrapolate for the school year, is approximately equivalent to what private schools spend on each student.

Come September, all twenty students were enrolled in ninth grade. This summer (2014), all twenty are still under our auspices in summer enrichment programs, and all twenty will be in good tenth-grade programs, including private boarding schools and demanding college-prep. schools. Virtually all twenty now see college as a given. In fact, we have created a bank account for each one of these students, so that upon graduation from high school, each student will have $2,500 for their next step, whether it be a vocational education, a community college, or a four-year college or university. The bank accounts have been powerful for the students and their families, not only in practical terms but also because the money conveys our belief that these young people can graduate from high school and take those next steps toward building satisfying careers and successful, self-sustaining lives.

What is perhaps most striking—because of its counterintuitive reality—is the buoyant and vital nature of the Lennox community. There is a pride that is almost palpable when you spend time in the neighborhood. Despite the poverty and unemployment and the sad, sorry list of social problems, there is an optimism and determination for a better future exhibited by the parents for their children. Given any reasonable opportunities, they can and will succeed. I've been inspired again and again by Jonathan Kozol's conclusion in his book *Savage Inequalities* and quote the passage here in full:

> Surely there is enough for everyone within this country. It is a tragedy that these good things are not widely shared. All our children ought to be allowed a stake in the enormous richness of America. Whether they were born to poor white Appalachians or to wealthy Texans, to poor black people in the Bronx or to rich people in Manhasset or Winnetka, they are all quite wonderful and innocent when they are small. We soil them needlessly.

Along with Kozol, I believe that this need not be so. Problems created by human beings can be solved by us. This thought continues to light a fire within me.

EPILOGUE

We are such stuff
as dreams are made on, and our little life
is rounded with a sleep.

—Shakespeare, *The Tempest*

SOMETIMES I AM ASKED WHAT I have learned these past years working with low-income, highly at-risk foster and incarcerated youth; with young men and women our society has virtually written off as uneducable and unworthy of serious investment; with boys and girls whose circumstances are so dire as to be deemed immedicable.

What I have learned is that these assumptions—be they conscious or not—are false. If you start with the premise that all children and young people are inherently valuable and potentially productive, then you seek to bring quality education to *all*.

Acting upon this premise, I have learned that quality education needs to be buttressed by encouragement, affection, and long-term commitment. The students referenced above need all the above to overcome a deep-seated sense of hopelessness that their poverty imposes upon them. "Hope," writes Emily Dickinson, "is the thing with feathers— / That perches in the soul— / And sings the tune without the words— / And never stops at all."

What gives these students hope is having someone believe in them. Relationship is the key. Once students have been given the sense that they are valued and that there are people committed to them for the long haul, they can then make up lost ground quickly; they can learn at a surprising rate. Foster children can go to and graduate from college; former incarcerated gang-bangers can redirect their lives; and poor children and youth can achieve goals that surprise even their families, teachers, and friends. We, society, sell them short way too soon. For me, seeing what they can do has been an inspiration and has fortified my college-liberal notions of what a powerful role the student's environment plays in his or her development. Environment combined with relationships—these are what matter.

As I have passed the three-quarters-of-a-century mark, I cannot help but sense time's winged chariot drawing near. I would like to keep working, like my mentor Herbert Zipper, into my eighties and even my nineties. But since none of us knows how much time we are to be allowed, I can only deal with projects a day, a week, a month at a time.

Ideally, I would like to see Coalition for Engaged Education (formerly New Visions Foundation) achieve such stability that my absence would not affect its ability to continue and to flourish. I would also hope to see our LENZ project become fully funded and sustainable—the well-being of thousands of poor children will be dramatically enhanced if we can provide such a legacy.

In addition, I would like to see a complete turnaround in California's juvenile justice system so that troubled youth receive respect, education, encouragement, rehabilitation, guidance, and long-term mentors upon release from the camps and lockup facilities.

I would also hope to see our Coalition for Educational Opportunity foster program flourishing in New York City, Brooklyn, Detroit, Seattle, and the San Francisco Bay area—this program works wonders with foster youth.

I hope to see my daughters' dreams—Anna's for ocean conservation and environmental sustainability and Emily's for improved treatment for at-risk children's emotional needs—more fully developed. The pride I feel for these two young warriors is immense; I am also deeply proud of their husbands' values and commitment. My two stepdaughters are an additional source of pride. Liesl is a superb harpist and teacher. Julie is a magnificent surgeon and professor of surgery, and her husband, Paul, is a world-renowned surgeon. As we watch them all do their work in the world, their mother and I can only smile. Watching our grandchildren grow and find their ways will be a day-to-day blessing for the time to come.

As I look back, excluding the blunders and inevitable mistakes we all make, mostly I feel proud of having created some innovative education programs—many that have "caught on" and have been incorporated in many schools. Of course, I am pleased to have helped create several schools. And I am proud of the books I have written, including this one. Finally, I have learned for myself the truism that most spiritual teachers over the centuries have taught: that happiness comes from helping others, and that this is what gives life meaning.

Finally, Mary Ann and I hope to continue our life-affirming work—which now spans more than a combined one hundred years. We would each like another fifty, but we will have to settle for whatever the fates allow. Herbert Zipper often said, "I want to be a good ancestor." Mary Ann and I echo that desire.

A PERSONAL, BRIEF, IDIOSYNCRATIC, AND
LIFE-CHANGING BIBLIOGRAPHY

Brinton, Crane: *The Shaping of Modern Thought*
Brooks, Cleanth: *The Well Wrought Urn*
Djilas, Milovan: *The New Class*
Ciardi, John: *How Does A Poem Mean?*
Hofstadter, Richard: *Anti-Intellectualism in American Life, The Paranoid Style in American Politics, Social Darwinism in American Thought*
Eliot, T.S.: *The Waste Land*
Frost, Robert: *Collected Poems*
Glaser, Elizabeth: *In the Absence of Angels*
Goldman, Eric: *Rendezvous with Destiny*
Hartz, Louis: *The Liberal Tradition in America*
Kazin, Alfred: *On Native Grounds*
Kessler, Rachael: *The Soul of Education*
Kozol, Jonathan: *Death at an Early Age, Savage Inequalities*
Levitt, Peter: *Fingerpainting on the Moon*
Link, Arthur S.: *American Epoch*
Niebuhr, Reinhold: *The Children of Light and the Children of Darkness*
Orwell, George: *Animal Farm, 1984*
Pearce, Joseph Chilton: *Magical Child*
Pease, Otis: *Blueberry Pie, The Progressive Era* (ed.)
Richards, I.A: *Practical Criticism*
Salinger, J.D: *The Catcher in the Rye*
Schlesinger, Arthur M., Jr.: *The Age of Roosevelt*
Thomas, Dylan: *Collected Poems*
Veblen, Thorstein: *The Theory of the Leisure Class*
Warren, Robert Penn: *All the King's Men, Collected Poems, Understanding Poetry*
Wickes, Frances: *The Inner World of Childhood*
Wilbur, Richard: *Collected Poems*
Wills-Hurwin, Davida: *A Time for Dancing*
Yeats, W.B.: *Collected Poems*
Zimmerman, J. & Coyle, V.: *The Way of Council*

The wind has changed; it is time to go.

—Evan S. Connell

ABOUT THE AUTHOR

Paul F. Cummins, renowned educator and founder, CEO, and President of the Coalition for Engaged Education (formerly New Visions Foundation), is committed to creating opportunities for all children to have equitable access to a quality education. He has founded and co-founded numerous schools including Crossroads School, New Roads School, Camino Nuevo Charter School, and New Village Charter School, as well as P.S. Arts, an NPO providing arts classes to children in Title I schools.

Cummins has published four books on education, a biography, two volumes of his original poetry, and two children's books. He has a forthcoming book entitled *Engaged Education: New Visions for Joy and Success in Learning.*